EGYPT

1. Lake Nasser.The great accumulation lake created by the High Dam of Aswan has resulted in ecological as well as economic disaster, in the view of many. The picture shows the changes in the water level which have had a harmful effect on life in the lake — a far cry from the Nasserian dream of verdant shores with flourishing fishing villages.

2. Wind and water shape the desert. A network of dry wadis create complex erosion patterns in the darkened sand of northern Sinai. (pp. 2-3)

3. Along the Red Sea coast the water is crystal clear. Coral and tropical fish thrive in a sea of emerald. Now a road runs all the way from Suez to the Egyptian-Sudanese border and luxury hotels and villas are springing up. (pp. 4-5)

4. Bedouin women in the north on a long, dull trip back to camp from the range where scanty scrub may be found. (pp. 6-7)

5. The best means of transport in Egypt, old and new: the camel and the helicopter. Many of Egypt's rulers have been military men, and the armed forces still play a major role in the country's political life. (pp. 8-9)

6. Modern roads cutting across the desert have taken the motor vehicle into camel territory. A highway completed in 1986 links Aswan with Abu Simbel, which can now be reached in three to four hours by car or bus. (pp. 10-11)

7. Palm groves sometimes look as old as the pyramids. Though not native to North Africa, the date palm came into Egypt with civilization itself. Apart from palms, the sunt tree (Acacia nilotica) is the most widespread. Figs, pomegranates, mulberries, citrus fruits and bananas are also widely grown. (pp. 12-13)

8. Peasant boys in traditional and universal garb run across a berseem field. This fodder grass is one of the main cash crops of the Fayyum, a fertile region often erroneously called an oasis, some 90 mi. from Cairo. (pp. 14-15)

9. Giza, the Muslim cemetery below the rock of Nazlet es-Simman, south of the Great Pyramids.

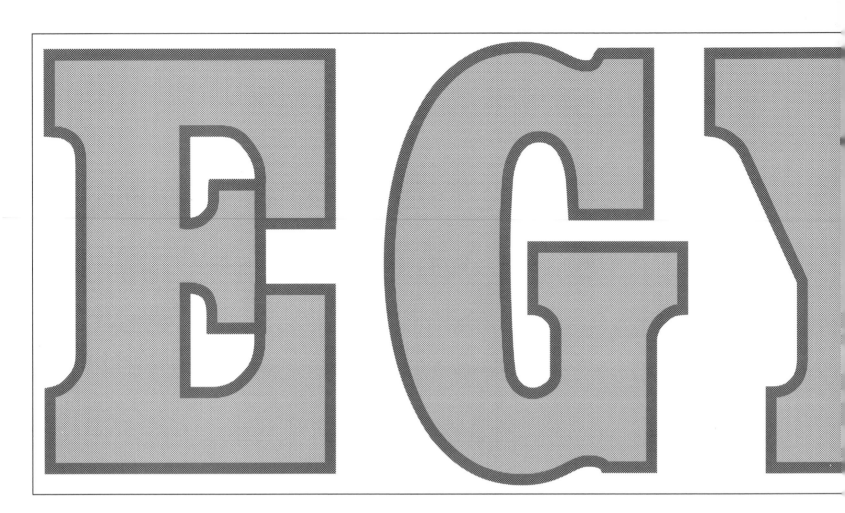

EGY

Text and captions

GIOVANNI CASELLI

Photographs

ALBERTO GUIDO ROSSI

FLINT RIVER

A Motovun Group Book
© Flint River Press Ltd. 1992

First published in the U.K. in 1992 by
FLINT RIVER PRESS Ltd.
26 Litchfield Street, London WC2H 9NJ

ISBN: 1 871489 12 1

Originated and developed by

Bato Tomasevic

Design

Gane Aleksic

Editor

Madge Phillips

Additional photographs by courtesy of

Scala Communications Inc.

nos. 4, 23, 24, 47, 52, 60, 62, 98, 104
105, 107, 112, 160, 173, 174

Drawings by Edward W. Lane taken from 'The Manners and Customs
of Modern Egyptians', first published in London in 1836.
Published by Everyman's Library in 1908.
Re-issued by J. M. Dent & Sons, London, 1963.

Typesetting by Avalon

Printed and bound in Slovenia by
DELO – Tiskarna, Ljubljana

CONTENTS

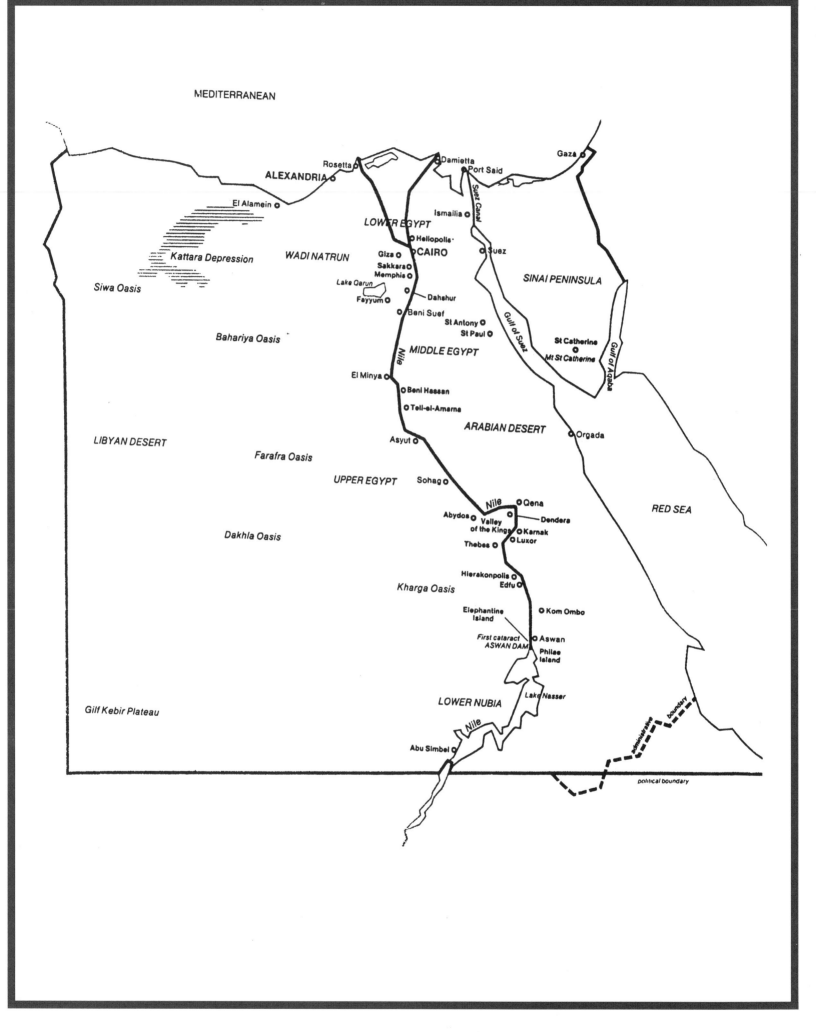

MEDITERRANEAN

Gaza

Damietta
Rosetta
ALEXANDRIA
Port Said

El Alamein
Ismailia
LOWER EGYPT
Suez Canal

Heliopolis
Giza CAIRO
Kattara Depression
WADI NATRUN
Suez
Sakkara
Memphis
SINAI PENINSULA
Siwa Oasis
Lake Qarun
Dahshur
Fayyum
Beni Suef

Bahariya Oasis
St Antony
St Paul
St Catherine
MIDDLE EGYPT
Nile
Mt St Catherine
El Minya
Gulf of Suez
Gulf of Aqaba
Beni Hassan
Tell-el-Amarna
ARABIAN DESERT
Orgada
LIBYAN DESERT
Asyut
Farafra Oasis
UPPER EGYPT
Sohag
RED SEA
Nile
Qena
Abydos
Dendera
Dakhla Oasis
Valley
of the Kings
Karnak
Thebes
Luxor
Hierakonpolis
Kharga Oasis
Edfu
Elephantine
Island
Kom Ombo
First cataract
Aswan
ASWAN DAM
Philae
Island
LOWER NUBIA
Lake Nasser
Gilf Kebir Plateau
Nile
Abu Simbel
Administrative boundary
political boundary

Introduction

Few civilizations in history have been so much admired and so thoroughly studied as the ancient Egyptian. There are thousands of people all over the world who are extremely knowledgeable about ancient Egypt and yet they may never have a chance to visit the country. Then, again, there are many visitors to Egypt who know all about its past but almost nothing of its present. Much more numerous than these are the 'ordinary' tourists who know relatively little about either the present or the past, yet feel an irresistible attraction towards it, flocking there in their thousands each year, to cruise down the Nile and gaze in wonder at the temples, pyramids and tombs.

The sheer size of ancient Egyptian monuments, their great number and the solidity of their construction have enabled them to withstand thousands of years of pillaging and vandalism. The handiwork of ancient Egyptian craftsmen and artists, the tombs, the debris of millennia of daily life, have largely survived, preserved by the dryness of the climate and the nature of the soil. There is probably more of the past than there is of the present in Egypt. The products of thousands of years of human labour during the age of the pharaohs still outnumber the products of human activity since that time. Hundreds of museums around the world cherish their Egyptian collections; not only Paris, London and New York, but also unexpected places such as Manchester and Turin boast major collections of Egyptian art and artifacts. Even so, under the burning sands of the Nile Valley, in the caves of Upper Egypt, countless treasures still await the spade and pick of the archaeologist.

Most armchair travellers have a mental picture of the country in which the glorious past quite overshadows the present. In reality Egypt goes far beyond any imagination or preconceived idea, particularly if the visitor does not confine himself to dead Egyptians — as novelist William Golding comments — and looks around at the vibrant, fascinating life that goes on in the cities, along the Nile and in the desert. It is precisely the intermingling and juxtaposition of ancient and modern, of different civilizations and traditions, that gives this land its unique fascination.

The Land and the People

Geography

Egypt is the land bridge and crossroads between Africa and Asia, while the Suez Canal joins the western and eastern seas. Its shape on the map is arbitrarily geometrical: an almost square patch in the north-east of the African continent. It covers an area of 387,390 sq. mi. — 1.8 times the size of France — but only 15,000 are suitable for habitation. West and south, the border follows a straight line, unrelated to physical features; to the north is the Mediterranean coast, also quite straight; to the east, the heart-shaped Sinai Peninsula, geographically in Asia, and the Red Sea coast form a rather more articulated border. The latter, following a line tilted north-west to south-east, is nothing like as dull as it looks on a map: rocky cliffs, inlets and harbours combine to give it both interest and beauty. Within this square, mostly flat, somewhat monotonous, desert area there is one striking feature: the great valley of the Nile, which flows northward through Egypt, almost parallel with the Red Sea coast, for some 900 mi. Fed by the tropical rains of Uganda and Rwanda, it crosses the largest desert of the planet for nearly 3,700 mi., its volume reduced by absorption and evaporation as it flows north, until it reaches the shores of the Mediterranean, where it spreads out in several branches across the vast expanse of silt known as the Delta. Historically, Egypt comprised the alluvial lands of the Nile north of the First Cataract at Aswan, originally divided into two cultural units along geographical lines: the Delta or Lower Egypt, and the valley between the present Cairo area and Aswan — Upper Egypt. The Nile Valley within Egypt is not, strictly speaking, a rift valley, like the Great Rift Valley of East Africa or the Jordan Valley. It is, nevertheless, entrenched between sandstone or limestone cliffs, which can be seen quite clearly for long stretches on either side by the traveller on a boat.

In the past, the Nile was navigable as far as the First Cataract, at Aswan, where massive granite boulders obstructed the river bed. Sailing along the river was easy: downstream boats were carried by the gentle current, and upstream the northerly winds, prevalent in summer, puffed out the white sails. East of the Nile lie the highlands of the Arabian Desert, a fractured part of the Arabian Peninsula, split off millions of years ago by the opening up of the Red Sea. To the west stretches the Libyan Desert, less high, equally arid, and broken by wadis. Few natural routes allow communication across those inhospitable, sun–scorched expanses of rock and sand. Eastward, it is possible to reach the Red Sea coast from Beni Suef in the north, from Qena, where the river comes closer to the coast, and from Aswan. Two main routes cross the Libyan Desert: one lies along the coast, just behind the sandy dunes; the other, largely defined by nature, runs far inland and connects a string of oases.

Without the Nile, Egypt, practically rainless, could have supported only a few thousand Bedouins. As it is, the country in 1990 had 54,139,000 inhabitants, 98 per cent of them living on the narrow strip of arable land, 15,000 sq. mi. in area, created by the silt carried by the regular flooding of the river produced by tropical rains far to the south. From Herodotus onwards, Egypt has been called the Gift of the Nile. Its great civilization could never have arisen without the beneficent and predictable waters of the river. Nor, indeed, would it have existed without the incessant toil of the Egyptian peasant. If the regular floods made settled life possible, their irregular volume sometimes had disastrous consequences: excess caused inundation of towns and villages; scarcity caused famine. It was the need to predict and control the floods that brought into being a well-organized and centralized state.

10. Ismailia, a mosque beside the Suez Canal. Lying on Lake Timsah, half way between Port Said and Suez, the town was founded by Ferdinand de Lesseps in 1863 while working on the construction of the Canal. From here, the Ismailia Canal runs westward to link up with the Nile, mostly following the same route as a pharaonic ship canal.

11. As the Delta builds up, extending further and further into the Mediterranean, fishermen's villages are the first to take hold on the marshland. (pp. 26-27)

12. Just north of Cairo the Nile divides into two branches, the Damietta (Dumyat) flowing east and the Rosetta (Rashid) flowing west into the Mediterranean. These branches are named after the ports at their mouths.

13. Port Said, the fourth largest town in Egypt. Located on the sea at the northern end of the Suez Canal, to which it owes its origins and importance, it was founded in 1859, when work began on the Canal, and named after the viceroy of that time.

14. An Australian sailing boat on the Nile. One may wonder whether it came all the way from Down Under by sea, or was transported by some other means.

15. *Fishing boats on the Red Sea coast, a region where tourism is rapidly developing thanks to its magnificent beaches and clear sea.*

16. The Suez Canal, begun in 1859 and officially opened ten years later, is 106 mi. long and up to 65 ft deep. Passage through it takes 15 to 18 hours as the speed of vessels is restricted to prevent the banks from crumbling.

31

17. Fort at Rosetta (Rashid), the major port
of Arab Egypt until Alexandria regained
importance in the nineteenth century. The
Rosetta Stone, now in the British Museum,
was found at Fort Rosetta in 1799. The
inscription on it in three languages
(hieroglyphic, Demotic and Greek) enabled
the French scholar Champollion to decipher
hieroglyphics in 1822.

18. Sailing boats on the Nile awaiting tourists who would like a cooling trip on the river after a day exploring the monuments of Upper Egypt. One vessel is appropriately named after the consort of Pharaoh Ramesses II.

19. Port Said (Bur Said), the gateway to the East, is more European in appearance than most Egyptian cities, with streets laid out in a grid system and few sights of historical interest.

20. A forerunner of the Suez Canal existed in pharaonic times, but led from the Nile to the Red Sea. The present Canal was opened in 1869, and from 1882 was administered by the British, who needed control of the waterways to India. In 1956 it was nationalized by President Nasser, an act which led to the Franco-British military intervention and the famous Suez Crisis. (pp. 34-35)

21. *A cruise vessel proceeds slowly up the Nile on a clear morning. On the far bank, banana plantations stretch behind the mud-brick peasant dwellings fringing the river.*

22. The town of Suez, on the northern tip of the Red Sea at the entrance to the Suez Canal. The site was settled in ancient times and the town itself founded in the fifteenth century, though it was of little importance until the construction of the Canal.

23. An increasingly rare sight in modern Egypt is this water-raising device called a 'shadouf', often seen in ancient Egyptian wall paintings — proof that good inventions die hard.

24. 'I would rather ride a donkey than any beast in the world. He goes briskly, he puts on no airs, he is docile, though opinionated. Satan himself could not scare him, and he is convenient — very convenient.' (Mark Twain)

25., 26. The felucca is still the best choice for a Nile cruise, even when the voyage is between high, muddy banks because of the lowering of the water level.

The 'final solution' of this problem was the Aswan High Dam, built between 1960 and 1970, which created a reservoir called Lake Nasser, 250 mi. in length, stretching well into Sudan. This dam, regulating the supply of water to the 560 mi. of the Nile Valley from Aswan to the Mediterranean, has put an end to the natural cycle of seasonal floods. The disastrous consequences of this tampering with nature will be described later.

Climate. There are two types of climate in Egypt: one, the desert type, absolutely dry and hot, which extends over most of the country; the other, a drier form of the Mediterranean climate, which prevails in the far north, particularly in the Delta area. Apart from occasional storms, in the desert region several years may pass with no rain at all. The mountains of the Arabian Desert, east of the Nile Valley, receive slightly more rain on account of their altitude. Cairo has 1.3 in. of rain annually, the wettest month being January, while Alexandria has 8 in., most of it in December.

Basically, there are only two seasons, one cooler and pleasant from November to April, the other, beginning in May, uncomfortably hot. The range of temperature is considerable, both diurnally and seasonally. In the Nile Valley summer temperatures can be extremely high: Aswan records a mean daily maximum of 41.7° C in June, though at night the thermometer can fall to 16° C. The warm Mediterranean Sea does little to mitigate the coastal temperature.

Among the least agreeable features of the climate is the *khamish,* a dust-laden south wind. Particularly in spring and summer, it can blow for several days on end, making life extremely uncomfortable. The sun becomes hazy and is often completely obscured by a dust so fine it penetrates everywhere and can ruin unprotected camera equipment.

Broadly speaking, Egypt has four main geographical regions.

The Eastern Desert, a long, narrow stretch of highland, lies between the Nile Valley and the Red Sea. The volcanic rocks of this region are weathered by the rains of ages past, by scorching heat and winds. Steep gorges slice through the rocks, often opening onto deep valleys running predominantly east to west. The highest of the mountains, Gebel Shayib, reaches 7,178 ft, but the average altitude is only 2,000 ft. The Red Sea coast is rugged, with few sheltered harbours and many coral reefs, beautiful and full of marine life, but extremely dangerous to shipping. Scanty rain keeps some of the wadis moist enough to sustain a small population of Bedouins, some farmers and some herdsmen. The only permanent settlements are on the coast and are associated with either mining or tourism: Quseir, Safaga and the largest, Hurghada.

The Sinai Peninsula starts out in the north as a broad coastal plain covered with sand dunes and rises gradually towards the south into a system of mountains culminating in the ancient Mt. Sinai and Gebel Katarin (8,650 ft). To the east, the massif descends abruptly to the Gulf of Aqaba, and to the west to a narrow coastal plain and the Gulf of Suez. The population of the Sinai is sparse and mainly settled along the coast.

The Western Desert, covering three-quarters of Egypt, is the most inhospitable desert in the world. Though hilly to the south, the area is mainly low-lying and has the large Qattara depression, 400 ft below sea level, in the north-west. Here is the great *erg* or sandy desert, fringed by desolate expanses of rocky desert, where only a small number of nomads can survive. The infrequent rains of the highlands to the south percolate under the desert to emerge further north, where there are a few oases, right in the geographical centre of Egypt. These are inhabited by largely self-sufficient communities which grow dates for export and cereals, fruit and vegetables for local consumption.

27. A Nile tourist boat cruises serenely along the river bordered by the mud-brick dwellings of banana growers.

The Fayyum depression owes its fertility not to its lake, Qaroon, which is salty, but to its proximity to the Nile, whose waters are conducted there by the Bahr el-Yussuf Canal. About two million people live in the beautiful oasis of Fayyum, noted for its citrus fruits, grapes and olives, apricots and figs. Its centre is Medinet el-Fayyum, where the rural population gathers on market days. Wheat and rice are also grown in this area, which is famous for its artifacts, poultry and pigeons. The oases of Dakhla and Kharga have likewise been increasing their cultivable areas and their populations in recent years under the scheme known as the New Valley Project.

The Nile Valley and Delta, the fourth geographical region, has always been of paramount importance to the life of Egypt. The river reaches the Mediterranean north of Cairo, fanning out into the sea, where it has built up the Delta by the accumulation of silt carried from as far south as the Ethiopian Highlands by the seasonal floods. This process has been brought to an end by the construction of the Aswan High Dam, which traps all the silt suspended in the water. The Delta has a maximum width of 150 mi. from Alexandria to Port Said and extends from the Mediterranean coast to Cairo for a distance of 100 mi. The area slopes gently towards the coast, where it is marshy and has a system of lagoons, some quite extensive. Originally the Nile branched into several streams, but today there are only two natural outlets, the Rosetta and the Damietta branches, while the rest are artificial drainage canals.

The need to control the Nile waters by damming, in order to feed a growing population and also to prevent periodic flood disasters, was recognized even in ancient times. The oldest dam seems to have been built near Helwan between 2950 and 2750 B.C. Unfortunately, this great project collapsed at the first test, resulting in a disaster of such a scale that no further attempt was made for another three thousand years. The earliest barrage across the Nile in modern history was built under Mohammed Ali Pasha at the start of the nineteenth century. Others followed later: Zifta in 1901, Asyut in 1902, Esna in 1908 and Nag Hammadi in 1930. The benefits were obvious: raising the water level facilitated the flow into irrigation canals, and the system prevented the escape of water into the sea in the low Nile

The Book of the Dead, Turin Egyptian Museum.

season. The biggest of the dams built before the Nasser Revolution was the Aswan Dam constructed by the British in 1903 and subsequently twice enlarged, in 1912 and 1934. The Aswan High Dam completed in 1970 dwarfs its predecessor. Located some four miles south of the old one, it has a high-water mark 200 ft higher. When full, the artificial basin is 250 mi. in length (180 mi. in Egypt, 70 mi. in Sudan). Its width varies from eight to 16 km. Although the silt is now completely captured within the basin, it will take centuries before its capacity is significantly diminished. Complete control over the flooding has thus been achieved. An additional 1,680,000 acres will be permanently irrigated, thereby increasing by a quarter the total area under irrigation. This means, for example, that an extra one million acres of rice can be grown. In addition to these benefits, the amount of electricity generated should be sufficient to meet the industrial and household needs of the entire country.

But there is another side to the picture. The inundation of such a large stretch of the Nile Valley entailed the relocation of many thousands of Nubians, who lost their homes and farmland. The inhabitants of the Wadi Halfa, alone, numbered 10,000. On the Egyptian side of the border, the creation of Lake Nasser has had less dire consequences for the local population: they were moved 30 mi. north to the Kom Ombo district and work mainly in sugar refineries. There is a scheme to expand the cultivated area of Kom Ombo by bringing water from the lake. The Sudanese Nubians, however, about 50,000 all told, were relocated nearly 60 mi. to the south-east, in the Khasm el-Girba district on the River Atbara, a different type of environment which made the traditional knowledge and skills of the peasants totally useless. Their situation has since been improved by the building of a dam there, making it possible to raise crops of the same kind as in the Wadi Halfa area.

Apart from the advantages already mentioned, the High Dam scheme was intended to improve navigation, increase cotton production by 30 per cent, and augment the food supply with a catch of up to 100,000 tons of fish a year from Lake Nasser. But the planners overlooked, miscalculated or disregarded a number of crucial factors, in the first place, the environmental consequences. The creation of a huge body of water has altered the climate of Upper Egypt, increasing the amount of moisture and causing rains in Aswan and along the upper valley of the Nile never previously recorded. As a result, monuments that survived millennia in arid conditions are now seen to be disintegrating and require special conservation treatment. Nor should it be forgotten that only the most spectacular of the monuments were saved from inundation, and that much of archaeological and cultural value was lost forever.

Another problem is that the dam is a very efficient silt trap, and it was the silt in the past that served both to fertilize and to desalinate the soil. Now, costly desalination plants and artificial fertilizers have to be used to achieve the same effects as the silt. In terms of expenditure, this exceeds all financial gains in other sectors deriving from the dam. Moreover, evaporation over such a vast surface in one of the hottest places on earth results in the loss of billions of tons of water.

There was, in fact, an alternative scheme to that of the High Dam, which was called the Jonglei Project. This involved the construction of a canal in the Sudan which would have considerably shortened the course of the Nile, thereby reducing its evaporation further south and bringing far more water into Egypt. But this project would have had no visible effect on the people in Egypt, and would not have served to the same extent to rally support for President Nasser and the spirit of nationalism.

Population

Most Egyptians live on the banks of the Nile. The majority are of Arab or Bedouin stock, descendants of the nomads of the Arabian Peninsula who conquered the region in the seventh century. Then there are Coptic and Muslim Egyptians, Berbers — originally from the western part of North Africa, Camites — mostly Nubians and other Nilotic peoples — from Equatorial Africa, and finally Gypsies, Abyssinians and Europeans. Over 90 per cent of the population speak Arabic as their mother tongue; 10 per cent are foreigners from Europe, Africa or other continents living in Egypt for business, employment or personal reasons.

Despite poverty, overcrowding, and the high infant mortality rate of 94 per thousand live births, the population is growing at a frightening pace: an annual increase of 2.8 per cent. Average life expectancy is now about fifty-seven years.

This factor, coupled with modernization of agriculture and shortage of arable land, has led to the rapid expansion of the cities, particularly Cairo, which now has 6.3 million inhabitants (17.5 million in the administrative area), and Alexandria with 2.8 million. Port Said (650,000) and Ismailia (450,000) are the next largest of 15 cities with over 100,000 inhabitants.

About 60 per cent of Egypt's population live in hamlets or villages, the remainder in towns and cities of over 25,000 inhabitants. Some 80 per cent are involved in agriculture, which occupies three million hectares of the arable land. The *fellah*, the poor farmer, often scrapes a living from less than an acre of land (0.4 hectares) and few are lucky enough to have five acres (two hectares). Fortunately, the climate allows more than one crop a year, the drawback being that the *fellah* does not enjoy the winter rest afforded the peasant in more northerly climes. He lives in a simple dwelling of mud-baked brick built by himself or his forebears. It is usually part of a village that has no discernible plan, and stands on a hillock called a *kom*, formed from the debris of earlier buildings, perhaps going back to ancient times. This elevation proved useful in the past as protection against floods.

Besides vegetables for household consumption and the market, the *fellah* raises poultry for eggs, rabbits and pigeons for meat and manure, perhaps a goat or two, a buffalo, and two skinny draught cows. Transport is provided by a donkey. His equipment is basic: a hoe, a rudimentary plough, a pitch-fork, a sickle, and a shovel for digging irrigation canals. His diet is frugal as he finds it preferable to sell his produce at the market. The main cash crop is cotton, which takes up most of the arable land available. Some is allocated for *berseem* (medic grass) to feed the donkey and other livestock. Luckily, this is fast growing and may be cut five times in one season. The tiny piece of land left is for vegetables and other food crops. The rich dark soil of the Nile Valley has always given high yields. In ancient times, barley, millet and emmer wheat were the main crops. Later, the Romans introduced bread wheat. Olives grew in the Delta 3000 B.C. and the date palm is indigenous to Egypt.

Flora and Fauna. There is a closeness between all the Mediterranean lands which history in recent centuries has tended to obscure. From earliest times the 'Inner Sea' was an avenue for trade, biological and cultural exchange, and communications between the lands around its shores. Long before human life appeared, the Mediterranean was a habitat for plants and animals with similar requirements. Thus, the biology of southern Europe has many similarities with that of North Africa, while the latter has little in common with nature south of the Sahara. The animals and plants of the Mediterranean world, which includes the Nile Valley, belong to the

zoogeographical region called Palaeo-arctic, while Africa south of the Sahara belongs to the Ethiopian region. In this respect, Egypt's indigenous fauna included species unknown in the sub-Saharan region, among them the pig, ox, goat and deer. During the warmer interglacial periods, Ethiopian flora and fauna, including early man, descended the Nile Valley and reached farther north than elsewhere on the continent.

Despite deterioration of the environment in recent decades due to overpopulation and pollution, the variety of fauna has not been much depleted. The lion has vanished and there are no longer monkeys living in the wild. In old paintings two varieties are frequently depicted: the green monkey (Cercopithecus aethiops), found nowadays only south of Khartoum, and the hamadryas baboon (Papio hamadryas), believed in ancient times to be the expression of the god Thoth, now found only beyond the border with Sudan.

Smaller creatures are found in abundance: many kinds of bat, other insect-eaters such as shrews and hedgehogs, and numerous rodent species, amongst them the Egyptian jerboa and kangaroo mouse. The carnivores include several varieties of dog. The Egyptian semi-wild dog, which the traveller will often see lazily crossing the road, causing traffic to slow down, is a Near Eastern breed crossed with the jackal (Canis aureus). A black variety of this jackal became identified with Anubis and other underworld deities. Foxes also come in several varieties, at least four of them, including the lovely tiny fennec, common in Egypt. No otters live in the Nile, but there are two kinds of weasel: one the large Egyptian variety, the other the desert striped weasel. The Egyptian mongoose and the genet are the two representatives of their species. They are close to the hyena, of which two types are present: the striped hyena, in the north, and the smaller aard-wolf, in the far south. The animal most people associate with Egypt is the cat. There are a number of wild breeds in the country, which is the homeland of our own domestic variety.

The ubiquitous pigeon is the most noticeable bird, many being raised domestically. Swallows nest on the ever higher banks of the Nile, while gannets and cormorants are found on the water's edge. Herons, storks and the little egret frequent the wet fields. Many types of falcon are also present.

And what about the dreaded Nile crocodile? Dead specimens can be seen hanging above doorways in Aswan and in farms in Upper Egypt, but these are presumably mummies since the creature is supposed to be extinct in this country. Among reptiles there are numerous snakes, some deadly poisonous, such as the cobra and viper.

The waters of the Nile, though polluted, are still rich in fish. The catfish, in fact, thrives in polluted water and takes over the territory of other, more delicate fish.

Ancient Egypt

If history is defined as the written record, then Egypt possesses the largest and oldest body of history of any country. Its annals begin with a list of prehistoric kings, their names known through oral tradition. Although there is still much argument and controversy among scholars over dating, it is now generally accepted that the First Dynasty was established in about 3200 B.C., the time when records of the main events of each year began to be written. Not only the duration of the king's reign, but also the quantity of flood water in the Nile were recorded. Only fragments of these annals survive, the earliest finely engraved on stone.

Another important document of Egyptian history is the Canon of Kings, fragments of which are preserved in Turin's Egyptian Museum. This covers a long line of dynasties extending over thousands of years. A wealth of collateral material, the extant monuments and the work of archaeologists generally confirm and authenticate these records.

A third document is the History of Manetho, written in Greek and compiled from all the available records that had survived down to the Greek period. Although the ptolemaic documents wrongly interpret the length of every reign, they are correct as far as the facts are concerned.

Throughout Egyptian history there is a wealth of detail that throws light on each period of prosperity. For the First Dynasty there are royal tombs and tables, and the recorded titles of hundreds of royal officials. In the Fourth to Sixth Dynasties, daily life was represented in innumerable reliefs and paintings on tomb walls, a 'strip cartoon' superior to that of any other age or country. The Twelfth Dynasty is known through stories concerning travel abroad, biographies, and pictures of daily life on feudal estates. The Eighteenth to Twentieth Dynasties, the best documented of all, have left hundreds of painted tombs in the Valleys of the Kings and Queens at Thebes. Most of the major monuments still in existence, with the exception of the Great Pyramids, belong to this Golden Age of Egypt's history.

Recent studies by British archaeologists have suggested a more recent date for the age of Tutankhamon, while making the Great Sphinx considerably older, but when contemplating a civilization that endured for thousands of years, a few centuries more or less seem immaterial to anyone but the specialist. If we now know that Stonehenge is older than the Pyramids, this does not detract or add anything either way: they remain two of the most extraordinary building achievements of mankind.

Even when the Sahara was not entirely desert, some 20,000 years ago in the Ice Ages, the Nile Valley in Upper Egypt offered a much more favourable proposition for a growing population, often in conflict over scarce food resources. Archaeological evidence indicates that as early as 18,000 years ago there was a noticeable increase in the numbers living on the narrow green strip along the Nile. At sites such as Wadi Kubbaniya, near Aswan, there appear to have been communities of some size that were increasingly capable of exploiting local food resources. Between 15,000 and 11,000 years ago came an era of plenty, a period of very abundant floods, when the green valley was alive with game, juicy fruits were always ready for the plucking in fragrant groves, and the murky waters teemed with fish.

In Nubia, on the banks of the upper Nile, an embryonic form of village life was already developing at this time, much earlier here than in the Middle East, or anywhere else in the world, for that matter. Qadan is one region of Nubia where grain collectors, or even cultivators, ground their wild varieties of corn on grindstones which have survived to this day. This unquestionable testimony of very early settled life is found on other sites, including the better-known Kom Omba, where local resources were used by three communities. At Kom Omba, life was settled all year round, people harvested wild grains and thoroughly exploited resources on the green plain, as well as in the surrounding desert and in the wooded fringe of the river.

In 12,000 B.C., at Esna local people harvested barley and kept animals, although it is impossible to tell in what degree of domestication.

To the north, in Lower Egypt, 7000 to 8000 years ago the Fayyum was a huge lake, its shores dotted with settled communities of fishermen and hunters. Harpoons and nets were used, probably from very specialized boats.

Intense use of wild cereals and selective hunting of grazing animals may have gradually led to the care of wild grasses by means of weeding and, perhaps, occasional provision of water, as well as to selective killing and breeding. After a while, actual sowing may have taken place to increase the density of these cereals at harvesting points, followed by periodic watering by means of small canals. From here to fully-fledged agriculture and animal husbandry was but a short step.

Although the place of origin of some domesticated crops and animal species is to be found in the Middle East, we cannot dismiss outright the possibility that agriculture and animal husbandry may have started with African varieties, first in the sub-Saharan region, as archaeological evidence now seems to be indicating. African crops, such as the yam, Guinea rice, sorghum, finger millet, teff, and others were used earlier than Middle Eastern varieties such as emmer wheat and barley.

This said, it is true that settled agriculturalists appeared in the Nile Valley much later than in Anatolia and the Fertile Crescent, indeed later than in the nearby Western or Libyan Desert. In the Fayyum, settled communities that grew crops were established from around 5000 B.C.

Hathor, the mother goddess, suckling the king.

The Predynastic Period

Around 4000 B.C., there emerged the culture known to historians as Predynastic, since it predates the sequence of recorded dynasties mentioned above. This is, in fact, a series of closely related cultures, identified by the style of pottery found as grave goods and named, after the sites which were first studied, as Badarian and Naqada I, II and III. The earliest sites are found along a 125-mile stretch of the Nile south of Asyut, extending further north and south in the course of time.

From the Naqada II period (3600 B.C.) copper is found in use for fashioning flat axes, knives and daggers. Baskets and linen were woven, and pottery was ornamented with painted decoration. During the fourth millennium B.C., there is evidence of steady development at sites such as Hierakonpolis, Naqada and Thinis, where the skill of craftsmanship implies a degree of specialization and stratification in society. In time, each of these pre-urban centres became the core area of a state which presumably had its own king and a special deity for worship.

Probably through contacts with the Near East, Egyptian neolithic culture developed the basic elements of civilization. The people of the Nile acquired building techniques involving stone and brick, cylinder seals for marking property, and a system of pictographic writing. Whether these ideas from abroad came to the Nile Valley through immigrants or trade contacts is impossible to say with certainty.

Two kingdoms emerged around 3500 B.C., one in Lower Egypt, which is to say, the Delta region, and the other in Upper Egypt, the Nile Valley. The earliest representation of a king is a relief on a macehead from Hierakonpolis, showing a ruler wearing the tall white crown of Upper Egypt. The first complete object of Egyptian art, a little later in date, is a slate cosmetics palette with reliefs carved on both sides, depicting a king, Narmer, identified by his name in the new hieroglyphic writing. On one side he is shown wearing the white crown of the southern kingdom, brandishing a mace over a captive before the falcon god, Horus. On the reverse, King Narmer, accompanied by priests and standard-bearers, is inspecting rows of headless corpses, presumably men slain or captured in battle. Significantly, he is here shown wearing the red crown of the north. These two reliefs clearly symbolize the triumph of the state-god of the south, Horus, and his earthly embodiment, King Narmer, over the northern kingdom. They also reflect the godlike status of the ruler, who is twice the size of the other figures.

The Early Dynastic Period

We know that around 3200 B.C. the state that had grown up in the south around Thinis gained control over the whole of the Nile Valley north of Aswan. The kings of Thinis formed the First Dynasty of historical Egypt, establishing themselves as pharaohs. Extensive trade began to develop soon after the creation of this large kingdom, crafts and industries flourished, and closer contacts were maintained with other centres of civilization, particularly Mesopotamia.

The union of Lower and Upper Egypt was regarded by the ancient Egyptians as the greatest event in history. According to the accepted chronology, this took place in 3150 B.C., when either Narmer or Menes proclaimed himself ruler of both kingdoms. The great King Menes diverted the course of the Nile to make the site for its capital, 'White Walls', known later as Memphis. Each king after Menes was crowned at Memphis and

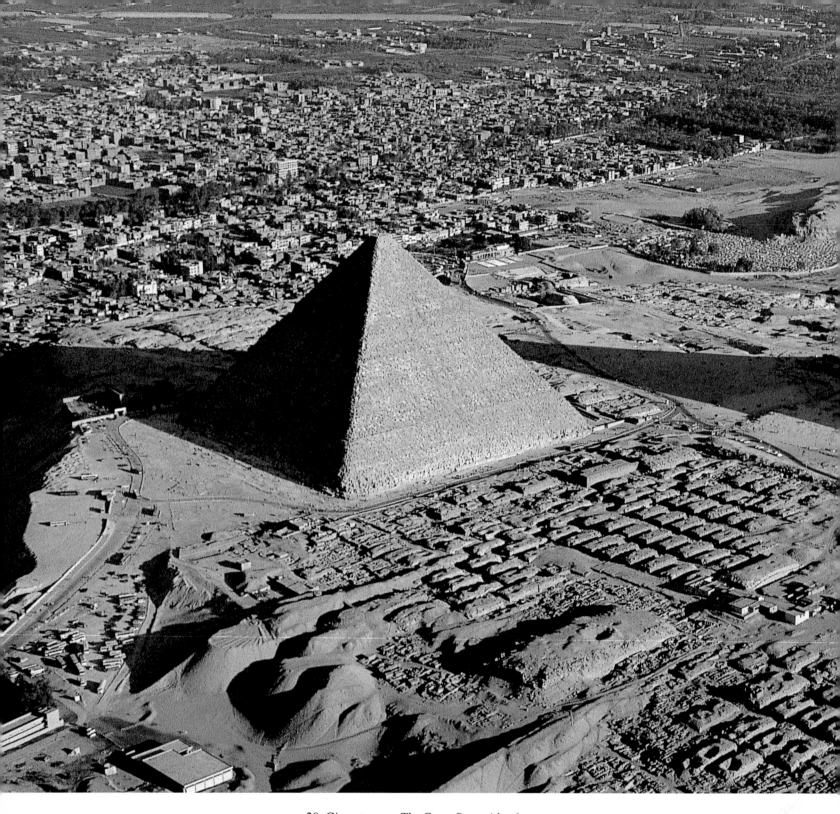

29. *Giza at sunset.The Great Pyramids of Cheops (Khufu), Cephren (Khephren) and Mycerinus (Menkaure) are better known in the West by their Greek than their Egyptian names. That of Cheops (left) is the largest pyramid in Egypt.*

30. Giza, the Great Pyramids of Mycerinus, Cephren and Cheops (left to right), the only one of the Seven Wonders of the World that remains to us. Pilgrims on their way to the Holy Land in the Middle Ages called them 'Joseph's granaries' and assumed they were diamond-shaped structures half buried underground. (pp. 52-53)

31. Dawn at Giza. The early morning may be chilly on the edge of the desert, but the 'baksheesh' boys with their faithful donkeys and camels are already in wait for early visitors.

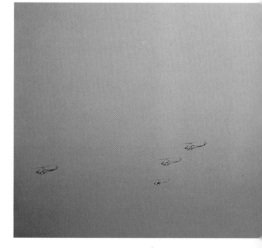

32. Egypt, ancient and modern. Helicopters flying past at dawn break the peace of the Great Pyramids.

33-35. Sunset on the fringe of the desert between Giza and Saqqara. The 'ships of the desert' cruise slowly along to their night's resting place after a long day in the blazing sun. For a few Egyptian pounds, the visitor can take an easy, though wobbly, ride among the pyramids — a memorable experience to tell the folks back home.

36. An amicable conversation at the end of a day of hard competition at Giza.

37. Made it to the top! The magnificent view is well worth the effort. The pyramid of Cheops, formerly 480 ft high and now some 10 ft less, is fairly easy to climb since the cladding that once made it smooth and shiny fell off long ago.

38. The Giza Sphinx was carved out of a natural outcrop of limestone composed of layers of hard and soft rock. As a result of erosion, these are clearly visible today. In the early nineteenth century, only the mighty head was visible because of the accumulation of sand. In 1925 the entire area was finally cleared and the monument restored. (pp. 60-61)

39. 'At our feet the bland Sphinx looked out upon the picture from her throne in the sands as placidly and pensively as she had looked upon its like full fifty centuries ago,' wrote Mark Twain. The American writer got it slightly wrong, however, for the Egyptian sphinx, associated with the pharaoh, was thought of as male, unlike the legendary Greek sphinx, whose name was borrowed by early Egyptologists. (pp. 62-63)

would walk the circuit of its walls during the coronation ceremony. The god of the new city was Ptah, who was believed to have created the land by the power of his word. The king's utterance was considered as creative as the word of Ptah, so that anything he cared to name would simply come into existence.

Unlike in other early civilizations, where the ruler was regarded as an instrument of the divinity, in Egypt he was believed to be a god himself — a typically African cultural attitude — and is always referred to as such in the earliest writings. Under an absolute ruler whose divine will was unquestioned, it was possible to organize land use, irrigation and control of the Nile floods, and to mobilize the labour force for the construction of vast projects, without danger of factions emerging to threaten the country's unity. King Menes is said to have started the building of dams on the Nile and the elaborate network of dykes and canals needed to exploit the flood water for irrigation.

To administer this enlarged kingdom and carry out the major construction projects, an efficient system of writing was needed. This was provided by the newly devised hieroglyphics and the invention of paper, obtained from papyrus pith. From the First Dynasty onwards, annual records were kept of kings, floods and crops. The movement of the stars and the life cycles of plants and animals were all carefully observed and described in calendars. Astronomy and mathematics soon came to regulate the relationships between celestial and earthly things, to dictate patterns and rules for building, irrigating, worshipping and feasting. A calendar based on twelve lunar months was developed from an older lunar calendar, and was subsequently improved. Each month had thirty days, with five extra days for feasting.

The kings of the First Dynasty, Aha, Zer, Den and others, seem to have waged war against their neighbours: the Libyans, and the peoples of Sinai, the Arabian Desert and Nubia. The most important of the few monuments from this period are their tombs, mainly brick-built, at Saqqara, near Memphis, and much further south at Abydos, in the region from which the dynasty originated. There seems to be much scholarly dispute as to where they were actually interred. One view holds that Saqqara, close to their new capital, is their burial place, but that they erected cenotaphs, 'empty graves', at Abydos to maintain their association with the region of their ancestors. Be that as it may, the First-Dynasty rulers, like their successors, were clearly much preoccupied with the construction during their lifetime of suitable burial places. The furniture, jewelry, stone vessels and other objects found in the royal tombs and palaces reveal the superb level of craftsmanship in this period.

The Second Dynasty (2980-2780 B.C.) seems to have been a period of struggle in which divine ascendancy shifted from the falcon god, Horus, to Seth, represented with the head of a jerboa or okapi, a spirit of nature associated with drought and violent storms, and then back to Horus again.

The Old Kingdom

While the kings of the first two dynasties were mainly concerned with the expansion of their realm, with public works and institutions, it is with the Third Dynasty (2780-2680 B.C.) that the country really became one nation. Some scholars regard this as the beginning of the Old Kingdom period, while others date it from the Fourth Dynasty, a century later.

The great King Zoser was the first to undermine the absolute superiority of the ruler when he allowed his architect the unprecedented honour of having his

40. Dramatic lighting creates the desired effect of the 'Father of Terror' (Abu el-Hawl), as the Giza Sphinx is often called. Guardian of the mortuary residence of Pharaoh Cephren, it was intended to keep tomb robbers at bay by its terrifying size (now 241 ft long and 65 ft high at the front).

65

statue erected in the sacred precincts of the god-king. Imhotep, a priest, physician, magician and poet, as well as an architect, became celebrated throughout Egypt. His fame increased over the centuries, until he was deified in the ptolemaic period. Twenty-three centuries after his death, he was worshipped as a god by the Egyptian Greeks. His outstanding achievement was the great step pyramid complex at Saqqara, covering an area 1,785 ft long and 909 ft wide. Enclosed within magnificent white limestone walls were the famous step pyramid, the first great Egyptian monument in stone, and several other buildings, where the Pharaoh's treasures were buried after his death.

With the Fourth Dynasty (c. 2680-2565 B.C.), records begin to get fuller and more accurate. This age has left remarkable examples of sculpture — some of the finest works in all ancient Egyptian art, reliefs, and wall-paintings. It is chiefly remembered, however, for the Great Pyramids of Giza built for the Pharaohs Cheops, Cephren and Mycerinus. Who can fail to be astonished by the vast scale of these monuments, the precision of their construction, and the skill needed to move their huge blocks of stone? Not to mention the vast expenditure of treasure and human labour involved. There is plentiful evidence that by the time of the Fifth Dynasty (2565-2420 B.C.) the position of the royal household, undermined by family strife, the huge expenditure on building projects, and other factors, was no longer unassailable. The building of some rock-cut tombs in the provinces shows that not all notable men wished to be buried near the court, and indicates a dangerous trend towards decentralization that ended with the collapse of the Old Kingdom in 2258 B.C.

Before then, pharaohs of the Sixth Dynasty waged some successful wars against neighbouring countries. The third of these, Pepy I, with his general Uni, conducted five military campaigns, attacking Palestine by land and sea. With his son, Mernera, his co-regent, he went to the First Cataract, to Elephantine (modern Aswan), to receive tribute from subjugated Nubian chieftains. After Mernera's death, his six-year-old son, Pepy II, ascended the throne to reign over Egypt for the next ninety-four years.

To all appearances, the Old Kingdom continued prosperous; it carried on its trade with the Syrian port of Byblos for the import of cedar wood and oil for embalming, and impressive royal monuments were raised of granite quarried around Aswan and shipped north. But in the course of his long reign Pepy II, a lenient ruler, would appear to have lost much of his control over the provincial nobility of Upper Egypt, far from the capital. For administrative purposes the country was divided into nomes, governed by nomarchs, and those in the south increasingly asserted their independence, building their own cemeteries instead of being interred in the royal burial ground. The death of the Pharaoh at the ripe old age of one hundred was the death-knell of the Old Kingdom. The country disintegrated, entering a period of upheavals named by historians the First Intermediate Period (2258-2052 B.C.).

At first there was anarchy, with the country splitting up into dozens of small warring kingdoms. The Seventh Dynasty had seventy kings and lasted seventy days in all. This system of having a new pharaoh each day was probably a political expedient adopted by the Memphites to break a political deadlock that ensued at the end of the Sixth Dynasty. After a time, the rulers of the Ninth and Tenth Dynasties, who were from Heracleopolis, not Memphis, managed to restore law and order and reconquer the Delta, invaded by desert tribes. However, they had only nominal control over Upper Egypt, where several local nomarchs held sway. Gradually, Thebes gained ascendancy in this

Re-Harakhty, who combined the qualities of the sun god Re (Ra) and Horus, the falcon god.

region, and eventually captured Heracleopolis in about 2052 B.C., reuniting the country and inaugurating the period of the Middle Kingdom.

The Middle Kingdom

The early pharaohs of the Eleventh Dynasty 'overlap' with the last Heracleopolitan rulers of the Tenth. From Thebes they extended their power first to the whole of Upper Egypt and later to the rest of the country, including the Delta. It was Mentuhotep II, fifth in the line, who finally broke all resistance. During his long reign, the obscure town of Thebes, formerly the chief city of a remote province, came to be regarded as the capital of the reunited country.

All the upheavals and tribulations of the preceding age may have contributed to the new spirit of experiment and, one might almost say, humanism that marked the Middle Kingdom, to judge by its literature and art. Mentuhotep II himself, like his immediate predecessors, was buried not in a pyramid but in a funerary temple, at Deir el-Bahari, consisting of a central building with two levels of terraced porticoes, approached by a ramp.

A new system of moral values can be detected in the writings, in which the ruler bore greater responsibility for his subjects, and there was increased concern for the individual, social justice, and human dignity. The idea of the equality of all men before the Creator appeared probably for the first time in history. This encompassed the idea that not only royalty would reach eternity; all human beings would be able to make the journey to the after-life. This right was granted by the god Osiris, ruler and judge of the world of the dead, whose cult, originating in the Delta, eventually spread all over Egypt. From the Eleventh Dynasty, its centre was established at Abydos, City of the Dead throughout ancient Egyptian history.

The powers and relationships of Osiris, his sister/wife Isis, and the numerous other gods of the huge and highly confusing ancient Egyptian pantheon underwent various transformations in the course of millennia, and defy any simple exegesis. It seems, though, from the religious literature of the Middle Kingdom, most notably the so-called Coffin texts, that the idea of a celestial afterlife gave way to the concept of an underworld, ruled over by Osiris, which is found in the New Kingdom *Book of the Dead*.

The founder of the Twelfth Dynasty (1991-1789 B.C.), Amenemhat I, had been the vizier (chief minister) of his predecessor. Having seized the throne, he established a new capital at Ith-tawe, near Memphis, from where he could control the north of the country better than from Thebes. He extended Egypt's control over Nubia, setting up a trading post at Karma, by the Third Cataract. His son, Sesostris I, followed in his father's footsteps and tightened the grip upon Nubia. He also attacked the Libyans, gaining control over the oases of the Western Desert. Later, Sesostris III made Lower Nubia an Egyptian province, while Amenemhat III reclaimed the Fayyum, building a great canal, the Bahr el-Yussuf, which is still one of the hydraulic wonders of Egypt, thus turning the region into one of the most fertile in the country.

The outstanding works of art of this age include the portrait statues of these two powerful kings, which like other stone and wooden sculpture of this dynasty are endowed with considerable psychological depth and characterization. From the Twelfth Dynasty we also have exquisite gold jewelry and objects in ivory and other precious materials, some of which show pronounced African influence, reflecting Egypt's southward expansion.

The brief reign of Queen Sebek-neferu-ra which ended this dynasty was followed by another age of political turmoil, the Second Intermediate

Anubis, jackal-headed god of the underworld, and Hathor.

Period (1786-1570 B.C.), as can be seen from the list of thirty kings, some contemporaries, of the Thirteenth and Fourteenth Dynasties, covering a period of about a century. In this weakened and divided state, Egypt succumbed without a blow (according to the historian Manetho) to foreign subjugation. As a consequence of upheavals in the Near East at this time, an Asiatic people known as the Hyksos, literally 'Rulers of Foreign Lands', settled in the Delta, where they established their capital at Hat-Uaret (Avaris). From here they gradually extended their sway over the whole country.

Their origins are still obscure: Josephus, the Jewish Roman historian, recognized them as the children of Israel. The Hyksos brought with them a number of innovations, among them the war chariot and body armour, and their own Syrian deity, which they identified with the Egyptian Seth. The monuments and scarabs of the Hyksos kings are found throughout Egypt and as far afield as Crete and Baghdad. Foreign rule lasted for a century and a half, until the princes of Thebes, having adopted Hyksos technology, took to their chariots, conquered Avaris, and chased the Hyksos all the way back to Palestine and Phoenicia. The Hyksos invasion had been the first serious threat to Egyptian sovereignty, but it was not to be the last.

The New Kingdom

The man who restored native rule by crushing the Hyksos was Ahmose I, founder of the glorious Eighteenth Dynasty. His son, Amenophis (Amenhotep) I, continued the reconstruction of the country and reconquered Nubia up to the Third Cataract. The dynasty produced a series of remarkable rulers, whose successful military campaigns greatly increased the country's territory and wealth. Egypt was now a military state, in which all power was vested in the monarch, his vizier and other court officials.

Tuthmosis I, the next pharaoh, was the first of the line to be buried in the Valley of the Kings at Thebes. His daughter, Queen Hatshepsut, co-regent towards the end of his reign, succeeded him and ruled for twenty years. Her magnificent temple at Deir el-Bahari is among the finest monuments of ancient Egypt. During her reign, a famous expedition was made to the land of Punt (probably on the Somali coast), recorded in beautiful friezes on the temple walls. When the Queen died and was succeeded by her co-regent and stepson, Tuthmosis III, there seems to have been a campaign of vandalism against her monuments and almost all portraits and records of her were defaced. This may reflect male reaction to the domination of such a powerful woman.

Under Tuthmosis III, Egypt's empire was extended over Lebanon, Syria and Mesopotamia — deeds recorded on his temple at Karnak, dedicated to Amon-Ra, now the dominant god. His grandson, Amenophis III, was another mighty builder, especially at Thebes, where he raised a sumptuous palace and a great funerary temple, of which only the Colossi of Memnon remain. In this period, Aten or Aton, the sun disk, was only one of the many deities of the Egyptian pantheon.

His son, Amenophis IV (1353-1335 B.C.), a physically feeble but intellectually gifted man, was to revolutionize Egyptian religion by imposing monotheism. Establishing Aten as the sole object of worship and himself as high priest, he suppressed all the other gods, closed down their temples, had their names erased from inscriptions and confiscated all the estates belonging to religious orders.

To counteract the influence of the priests of Amon, who had gained political status in Thebes, he decided to move his capital to Middle Egypt. At Tell el Amarna, half way between Cairo and Luxor, he had a new city built, named Akhentaten ('Horizon of Aten'), to which he moved his court in the fifth or sixth year of his reign. He changed his own name to Akhenaten ('He who serves Aten'), and that of his consort Nefertiti (Nofretete), whose beauty is immortalized in the famous painted bust in the Berlin Egyptian Museum. The greater emphasis on naturalism in art is exemplified in the equally famous colossal statue and head of Akhenaten from Karnak, now in the Cairo Museum, which shows the revolutionary Pharaoh as being ill-shapen, with a long thin face, thick lips and slanting eyes. It is believed that it was the King himself who set the new trend in art, in keeping with his propagation of a religion based on nature and the creative force of the sun. Worship of the sun disk Aten consisted simply of offering fruit and flowers on an altar in the open air.

Amon himself was a solar deity, having become assimilated in time with Ra, the sun god, but he was only one among many, albeit lesser divinities, in this period. In pictorial representations he was given anthropomorphic form, whereas Aten was simply the solar disk.

Despite all the efforts of this remarkable ruler, monotheism failed to appeal to the masses and was abhorred by the priesthood of Amon and all conservative elements in society. It is believed that Akhenaten had no son and was succeeded in turn by two sons-in-law. The second of these, Tutankhamon (1333-1323 B.C.), who ascended the throne at the age of eight or nine and died at eighteen, is among the most famous names of ancient Egyptian history, thanks to the finding early in this century of his tomb intact with all its magnificent treasures — one of the archaeological discoveries that has most captured the popular imagination. The fact that these were found in the relatively small tomb of a minor pharaoh makes it clear what must have been lost over the ages by the plundering of the tombs of much more important rulers — despite all the elaborate precautions against grave-robbers.

Both these successors of Akhenaten were married to his daughters, so there was some reluctance to suppress the worship of Aten outright. This was done by the next ruler, Horemheb, a general who had served under Akhenaten.

The Nineteenth Dynasty that followed (c. 1320-c.1200), together with the Twentieth, is known as the age of the Ramessides. During his sixty-seven years on the throne, Ramesses II 'the Great' is said to have filled Egypt and Nubia with monuments, along them the temples of Abu Simbel and the Great Hall at Karnak. Impressive though they are, surpassing in scale and number anything built before or after by a single ruler, the monuments of Ramesses II show excessive emphasis on size at the expense of refinement of craftsmanship.

Ramesses II moved the capital to the Delta, the region from which the dynasty probably originated, whence he waged war against the Hittites, who had retaken Syria. His battle against them at Kadesh and his personal heroism are vividly depicted on the walls of his great temples. During his twenty-first year on the throne, Ramesses II entered into a non-aggression pact with the Hittite King Hattusil, sealed by marriage to his daughter. A few years later the Hittite empire was to fall to the mysterious Indo-European Sea Peoples, who had swept down from the Balkan and Black Sea regions, through Greece, into Asia Minor. It was Ramesses II's successor, Merenptah, who had to face them when they reached the borders of Egypt. His army managed to defeat them in a bloody battle that left 9,000 dead, and the Pharaoh subsequently went on to recapture many provinces of Syria and Palestine.

After his death, a period of anarchy with five short reigns was followed by the accession of Sety-nekt, founder of the Twentieth Dynasty (1197-1085 B.C.). His son, Ramesses III, the last great pharaoh of ancient Egypt, was a brilliant military leader and administrator, who reorganized the government and divided the population into classes: palace officials, nobles, soldiers and artisans. The two senior 'civil servants', in charge of the judiciary, records, treasury and all public services, were the viziers, one at Thebes for the southern regions, and one at Heliopolis for the north. There was also a viceroy for Nubia, who held the titles 'Overseer of the Southern Land' and 'Royal Son of Kush'. The pharaohs did not much interfere in the government of the Asian provinces, but extracted heavy tribute from them, the main source of Egyptian wealth at this time.

It was during the New Kingdom that a professional army was first established, mostly garrisoned in the Delta and Lower Egypt, since external danger came primarily from the north. The commander in chief was usually of royal birth. Ramesses III, called the 'Egyptian Napoleon' by French scholars, had to repel renewed attacks by the Sea Peoples, who this time returned in greater numbers and posed a threat to Egypt's very survival as an independent state. He also waged successful campaigns against the Libyans. The Pharaoh's funerary temple at Medinet Habu, Thebes West, is his great legacy in stone: the deeds of the saviour of Egypt are recorded with amazing accuracy by the splendid reliefs on its walls.

At home, Ramesses III was beset towards the end of his reign by problems that have a contemporary ring: high inflation, strikes, economic corruption, increased crime (in this case, the robbing of royal tombs), and political instability. These problems became more acute under his successors, who were all called Ramesses, probably in his honour, but were far less capable. Decadence set in, and gradually the priests of Thebes acquired more and more power, as they always did in the time of weak rulers.

The Late Dynastic Period

The centuries from the accession of the Twenty-first Dynasty (c.1085 B.C.) until the conquest of Egypt by Alexander the Great (332 B.C.) are a period of decline, when feeble sovereigns were forced to share power with a growing number of almost independent dynasties. Internal anarchy resulted in the loss of prestige and domination abroad.

After the Ramesside age, a general named Herihor made himself high priest of Amon at Thebes and became the first in a line of priest kings who controlled the south of the country. They shared power, relatively amicably it seems, with the princes of Tanis (Avaris) in the Delta, where Smendes was the founder of the Tanite Twenty-first Dynasty. The Bible tells us that a Tanite princess was given in marriage to Solomon, an indication of the power and prestige of the kingdom of Israel at this time.

Around 950 B.C., Sheshonq I, a prince of Libyan origin, founded the Twenty-second Dynasty. This is known as Bubastite from its capital, Bubastis, in the Delta, a region long before infiltrated by Libyans, who were prominent in the army. This fresh blood seems to have revived Egypt's flagging fortunes for a while. Sheshonq is known to have entered Palestine in c.930 B.C., after the death of Solomon, sacked Jerusalem and carried off the treasures of the Temple. The Bubastite rulers managed to keep the country unified for a century, ensuring control of the south by appointing a member of the royal family as high priest of Amon at Thebes, but then the familiar pattern was repeated. Civil war broke out and a rival Twenty-third Dynasty was set-up, ruling parallel for some eighty years.

Bes, god of music and dance, and protector of mothers-to-be and infants.

By this time the Assyrian empire was again in the ascendant and encroaching westward. Faced by this menace, the petty rulers of the Delta united under Tef-nekt, prince of Sais, founder of the brief Twenty-fourth Dynasty. His son, King Bakenrenef (Bocchoris), made a pact with the Jews, but their allied armies were defeated by Sargon II in 720 B.C. At the same time, danger loomed in the south from the Kushite rulers of the Sudan (which the Greeks called Ethiopia and the Romans Nubia). King Piankhy or Piye of Kush took advantage of the situation to invade Upper Egypt, inaugurating the Twenty-fifth (Kushite) Dynasty (730-656 B.C.), which in the reign of his successor, Shabako, gained control over Lower Egypt as well. But after half a century of relative prosperity, disaster struck in the shape of the mighty Assyrian war machine. In 671 B.C. Esarhaddon captured Memphis, and in 663 B.C. Ashurbanipal sacked Thebes.

Egypt was delivered from the Assyrians and the Kushites by the ruler of Sais and Memphis, Psamtik I, founder of the Twenty-sixth Dynasty (664-525 B.C.), during which the country experienced its last period of brilliance. These Saite rulers were certainly aided by the fact that the Assyrian empire had by now become overextended and weakened by revolts in Babylon, Elam and Arabia. With the help of Greek mercenaries, Psamtik, who had been an Assyrian vassal, defeated and drove out the Assyrians in 658 B.C. In the fifty years of his reign, the economy revived and Upper Egypt was turned into a huge granary. But the centre of power and economic activity was now in the north, closer to the Mediterranean and its trade. The supremacy of Thebes in religious and political life was finally over. The reawakened national spirit led to a revival of the spiritual, intellectual and artistic life, with artists turning for inspiration to the great works of the Old and Middle Kingdoms. The highly expressive portraiture of this period was to be much admired and copied by the Romans.

Closer contacts with the Greeks were established: Psamtik II relied on Greek mercenaries as officers in the army and a fleet of Greek triremes was procured. In 565 B.C. Naukratis, a Greek free port, was established in the Delta. But their influence seems to have been mostly confined to military, maritime and mercantile matters, for there is scant trace of any Greek imprint on art or thought until the ptolemaic period. Rather the reverse, for the Greeks learnt much from the science and ideas of this ancient civilization. According to Herodotus, an attempt was made at this time to complete a canal to connect the Mediterranean and Red Seas — a forerunner of the Suez Canal.

This final flowering was dramatically cut short in 525 B.C. by the invasion of Egypt by Cambyses, ruler of Persia, the new super power, which had recently crushed Babylonia and was rapidly expanding its empire. Proclaiming himself pharaoh, Cambyses founded the Twenty-seventh (Persian) Dynasty, but for most of the next two centuries, the country was in fact no more than a satrapy of the Persian empire. After a successful revolt against Darius II, there was a period (404-341 B.C.) when the last three Egyptian dynasties managed to maintain independence. Kings Nectanebo I and II of the Thirtieth Dynasty were the last great builders of ancient Egypt. The latter was defeated by a fresh Persian invasion and is said to have fled to Nubia, thus ending ignominiously three millennia of pharaonic rule.

The Ptolemies

When Alexander the Great of Macedon entered Egypt in 332 B.C., after defeating the Persian, Darius III, at Issus, he was welcomed as a

41. Central Sinai. There are no permanent
watercourses in the whole of the peninsula,
but during a rare fall of rain, the wadis fill
up and water rushes through the gorges,
carrying with it tons of debris.

saviour. With characteristic decisiveness and speed, he reorganized the country, placing Greeks in all important posts, but respecting the institutions and religion of the natives. He paid a visit to the oracle of Amon in the oasis of Siwa, where the god acknowledged him as his son and foretold that he would conquer the world. For a new capital he chose a site on the coast, where the foundations of Alexandria were laid. After only six months of frenetic activity, he left for the Orient, where he died nine years later. His body was brought back for burial in Alexandria, the great city that is the most enduring testimony to his incredible exploits, though his mausoleum, the Soma, has not survived.

After Alexander's death, three of his generals split the huge empire among them and three dynasties of Hellenic kings emerged: the Antigonids in Macedonia, Alexander's homeland, the Seleucids in Persia, and the Ptolemies in Egypt. Ptolemy, son of Lagus, proclaimed himself king or pharaoh in 305 B.C., and his descendants ruled the country for the next three centuries. These Greek rulers adopted all the trappings and the religion of the pharaohs, though in the early period the culture of Alexandria was exclusively Greek.

The city became famous throughout the ancient world for its university, its library, its museum, and the Pharos lighthouse, one of the 'Seven Wonders'. As the centre of the civilized world at that time, Alexandria attracted the greatest philosophers and scientists of the age. Many of the foremost writers, scientists and intellectuals of the Hellenic world were teachers, researchers or librarians at the Mouseion, House of the Muses, and the Bibliotheka, the largest 'storehouse' of ancient knowledge, with perhaps 700,000 volumes. Most of these scholars were supported by the royal treasury.

The Ptolemies engaged in very costly plans for the country's defence. A large fleet was needed to protect the Mediterranean coast, and forts and walls were raised to safeguard the southern border from Nubian attacks. Elephants were captured in Ethiopia for use in warfare, their trainers being brought from India. Trade flourished: the timber required for shipbuilding was imported from the Aegean islands, iron and other commodities from further afield. The need for imports led to the growth of exports of African products such as ivory, gold and ostrich eggs. From across the Indian Ocean and up the Red Sea came hardwoods, dyes, silks and precious stones, which were all worked in Alexandria and then exported to Greece, Italy and the Black Sea region. The manufacture of papyrus, and also of wool, linen and glass, were important industries, as was the working of gold, silver and bronze. Banking also thrived: the banks of Alexandria had branches all over Egypt.

There can have been no shortage of labour for, according to the Greek historian Diodorus, the population in the reign of Ptolemy I was around seven millions, the vast majority, of course, tilling the land. All the rulers and officials were foreign, and the country was an immigrant's paradise. Colonies of veteran soldiers, mostly of Greek extraction, were established in all parts of Egypt, while the native population was for the most part reduced to the role of peasants and labourers. With a few exceptions, Egyptians never regained access to power and wealth until the middle of the nineteenth century. There was, however, considerable intermarriage, and after the revolt of the natives in the reign of Ptolemy V, Greek and Egyptian elements became closely intermingled.

In this age, many novelties reached Egypt from all over the known world, and certain aspects of Egyptian culture spread over the Hellenized world. Ptolemy I instituted the state worship of a triad of deities: Serapis,

42. Western Sinai, with the Red Sea on the right. Here, the eroded massif descends to a flat coastal plain. On either side of the main road are traces of ancient settlements.

43. North-west Sinai, a sandy region
intersected by dry river valleys, carved out
by rare but violent rainfalls in ages past.

44. The Sinai Peninsula, wedged between
Africa and Asia, is mostly barren wasteland,
treeless and inhospitable. It is the home of
several Bedouin communities, although their
populations are gradually dwindling.

45. *Mount Sinai. On the summit of the Gebel Musa peak stands a chapel dedicated to the Holy Trinity.*

46. *The holy monastery of St Katherine in southern Sinai, the most important Christian monument in Egypt. Set in the Wadi el-Deir, 5,150 ft above the valley floor, it is close to Mount Sinai, traditionally considered to be the place where Moses received the Ten Commandments. Hermits were already living in the lonely valley in 337, when Helena, mother of Emperor Constantine the Great, ordered the building*

of a sanctuary here, on what was believed to be the site of the biblical Burning Bush. A monastery renowned for its huge manuscript collection has flourished here ever since.

47. *The view from Mount St Katherine (Gebel Katarin), the highest peak of mountainous southern Sinai (8,650 ft). This desolate yet beautiful area is thought to be the southernmost point reached by the Israelites in their forty-year wanderings. (pp. 80-81)*

48. *Lake Nasser, the artificial lake formed by the Nile waters after the building of the Aswan High Dam, is some 250 mi. in length and stretches well into neighbouring Sudan. (pp. 82-83)*

49. Islands in the basin between the Old and High Dams at Aswan. Here was the First Cataract, the end of the world for the earliest Egyptians. Some of these, such as Elephantine and Kitchener's Islands, are real Gardens of Eden, with all manner of lush vegetation. (pp. 84-85)

50. The Hurghada Sheraton Hotel provides luxurious accommodation for visitors to this growing Red Sea resort, 245 mi. south of Suez. Its attractions include wonderful sandy beaches, superb conditions for underwater fishing and snorkeling, and year-round sunshine.

51. In the past, most European and American visitors came to Egypt for a leisurely winter cruise on the Nile, with excursions on shore to view the monuments. Today, the Mediterranean and Red Sea coasts with picturesque small ports and fishing villages are also attracting foreign tourists.

the Sacred Bull of Apis, identified with Osiris and Zeus, his wife Isis, and son Horus (Harpocrates). This concept of the divine Father, Mother and Son was to be carried over into Christianity a few centuries later. The main temple of this religion was the Serapeion in Alexandria, nothing of which survives. The cult spread to the Aegean, elsewhere in Europe, and India, and in the Christian era, the statue of Isis in Greek robes came to be worshipped as the Mother of Christ.

Like the religion, the art of the ptolemaic period was something of a hybrid. To gain the respect and sympathy of their subjects, the Ptolemies continued the pharaonic tradition of building splendid temples, such as those at Edfu and Dendera, and the Isis temple on the little island of Philae at the First Cataract, completed in the Roman period.

With all power concentrated at the court, intrigue and murder became a regular feature of the struggle for succession to the throne. By and large, the queens enjoyed more power and respect than the kings. Cleopatra VII, last of the ptolemaic rulers, endeavoured to keep the throne and maintain Egyptian independence through liaisons with Julius Caesar and Mark Anthony, representatives of the now dominant world power, Rome, which had been interfering in Egyptian politics for the past century or more. Unfortunately, she chose the wrong side in the Roman power struggle, and in 30 B.C. Octavian (later Augustus) invaded the country to defeat his rival, Mark Anthony, at Actium. In one version of the story, to which Shakespeare subscribed, at a crucial point of this sea battle, Cleopatra panicked and ordered the Egyptian vessels to withdraw, with disastrous consequences. Shortly after, besieged by Octavian in Alexandria, she committed suicide.

Roman and Byzantine Rule

For the next six centuries Egypt was a province of the great empire ruled from Rome and later Byzantium (Constantinople). Like the Ptolemies he replaced, Emperor Augustus treated the country as his personal domain, free from any interference by the Senate. Aware of the vital importance of Egyptian grain to feed Rome, Augustus decreed that no senator could set foot in the country without imperial permission. In this way he intended to prevent any rebellious general from holding Rome to ransom by threatening to cut off its staple food supply. The country was thenceforth governed by a carefully-selected prefect, the emperor's personal representative, who in a sense replaced the old kings.

The religion and customs of the inhabitants were for the most part respected, though Romans gradually took over the administration. The first prefect, Cornelius Gallus, secured Roman rule in Upper Egypt as far as Aswan. There was, however, a substantial difference between the ptolemaic and Roman administrations: whereas the wealth produced in Egypt had previously remained in the country with the ruling family, now much of it was carried off to Rome. This fact, coupled with periodic revolts and upheavals, led in time to poverty and even starvation.

One source of trouble was the quarrels between the Greeks and the Jews, whom Augustus had given equal privileges. The Jewish community in Egypt had long been very numerous. In Alexandria, one of the three (later four) main sectors of the city was the Jewish quarter, which was, in fact, the largest Jewish urban community in the world. The great Jewish revolt and massacre of the Greeks in the reign of Trajan was followed by several months of fighting against the Roman forces, ending in the virtual annihilation of the Alexandrian Jews. The city's population was also

52. A student of the Wissa Wassef Art Shool at Giza. Blue eyes are not so unusual in a country that has been visited by innumerable invaders.

decimated in A.D. 215, when Emperor Caracalla, in revenge for an insult, ordered the massacre of all males of military age.

Egypt, like other provinces, was affected by times of crisis in the empire when the imperial throne was contested and central control slackened. At one point, in the third century, it was invaded by Queen Zenobia of Palmyra, but Probus, the first governor of Egypt to be proclaimed emperor by the troops, soon restored Roman rule, which was maintained, apart from a Persian interlude, until the Arab conquest in 639.

Christian Egypt

Christianity very early on attracted numerous adherents in Egypt among Greeks, Jews and Egyptians. This can be seen from records of their persecution in the third and early fourth centuries by various Roman emperors, starting with Septimius Severus in A.D. 202, when he dissolved the celebrated School of Alexandria, the first Christian university. These persecutions continued until the Edict of Milan (313), decreeing freedom of worship throughout the empire. They seem, however, rather to have strengthened the Egyptian Church, founded according to tradition by St Mark, and headed by the Patriarch of Alexandria. By the middle of the fourth century, the new faith was well established throughout the country. One of the early Fathers of the Church, Athanasius, estimated in 339 that the number of Egyptian bishops was close to one hundred. Nevertheless, worship of the old gods, banned by the Edict of Theodosius in 392, continued, especially in Upper Egypt, until at least the time of the Arab conquest.

The name Coptic for the native Egyptian Church, and the word Copt, used today for its followers, derives from the Greek name for the country *Aegyptos*, corrupted by the Arabs to Gyptos/Coptos/Copts. The ancient Egyptians called the country *Kemi*, land of the black earth, while the Arabs adopted, and still use, the old Asian appellation, *Misr*.

The success of the new religion, not the only one to enter the country in this age, can perhaps be explained by the failure of polytheism to satisfy the needs of people in those uncertain times for a dogmatic faith that taught with absolute certainty what was right and wrong, for a religion of unquestionable truths that could provide a firm basis for belief. But human nature being what it is, the teachings of Christianity were soon the subject of varying interpretations. Arianism, named after Arius, an Alexandrian presbyter, and condemned as a heresy at the Council of Nicaea (325), denied the divinity of Christ, and the Nestorian heresy, a century later, questioned Mary's title of Mother of God. It was the patriarchs of Alexandria who were the main champions of orthodoxy against such 'deviant' views. Their city was for long considered the second centre of Christianity, after Rome, until supplanted by Constantinople.

In the fifth century, the Egyptian Church opted for Monophysitism, which denied the two-fold nature of Christ, human and divine, and asserted that he had a single nature with two aspects. While this may seem like hairsplitting at this distance in time, in the reign of Emperor Justinian it led to the slaughter of perhaps 200,000 Egyptians who refused to renounce this belief. Monophysitism, having become a symbol of national resistance, eventually prevailed, causing a schism between the Egyptian (Coptic) Church and other Christian Churches that survives to this day.

Egypt's great contribution to Christianity is monasticism, which probably had its roots in ancient Egypt, where anchorites are known to have taken to the desert to contemplate Amon from as early as the Nineteenth Dynasty, judging by graffiti in the Theban hills. Escape from persecution, taxation and other ills under Roman and Byzantine rule must have encouraged many Christian converts in Egypt to 'opt out' of society and lead a life of solitude, abstinence and prayer.

The concept of *anchoresis*, applied both to a hermit or anchorite and to an outlaw, often a man on the run from a tax-collector, seems to indicate that the roots of this tradition lay in dissatisfaction with the establishment.

Though there had earlier been Christian hermits in Egypt, notably Paul of Thebes, the father of the monastic way of life is considered to be St Anthony, who in the latter half of the third century went to live in seclusion in an abandoned fort on the east bank of the Nile, opposite the Fayyum. As his fame spread, many other ascetics came to live in the caves and rocks

Relief of the Virgin Mary suckling the infant Jesus, on a gravestone from Fayyum, fifth-sixth century.

around the fort and seek his guidance. After some twenty years, Anthony emerged from his retreat and set about organizing their life, thus inaugurating Christian monasticism.

But whereas Antonian monasticism, which had become prevalent in middle and lower Egypt, retained many eremetical features, further south St Pachomius established a much more organized system. In about 320 he set up the first cenobium or monastery proper near Dendera. This was a close-knit community governed by a multitude of rules in which the monks worshipped and took their meals together, and engaged in organized work. Before his death in 346, he had founded another nine monasteries for men and one for women. Pachomius, in fact, created the first religious order, with the abbot of the chief monastery serving as the superior-general.

Both models of the ascetic life spread to Europe and the Near East. In 340, St Athanasius, Bishop of Alexandria, took the idea to Rome, where his *Vita Antonii* was soon translated into Latin. The more austere, eremetical Antonian type was at first more widely accepted in the West, but in time it was the cenobitic way of life that predominated. St Basil, founder of monasticism in the Greek cultural sphere, inclined rather to the Pachomian model, laying down the rules followed by Eastern Christian monasticism ever since. The Rule of St Basil in its turn influenced that of St Benedict. It is interesting to note that Pachomius, who had been trained in the Egyptian literary tradition and was already twenty when he became a Christian, based the organization of his monastic communities on that of the ancient Egyptian priesthood, dividing them into families and then houses of monks who followed similar occupations. The Pachomian Rule likewise lays down the forty qualities of the ideal monastic leader, twenty of them drawn from the Bible and twenty from pharaonic tradition, expressed in a gnomic form reminiscent of the *Book of the Dead*.

The astonishing growth of monasticism can be judged by the fact that by the reign of Emperor Valens (364-378) such a large proportion of the population had taken vows that it became necessary to abolish the monks' privilege of exemption from military service. In these early centuries of Christianity, Egypt enjoyed enormous prestige throughout Christendom and was visited by pilgrims come to see the 'home of monks' and venerate the 'living saints'. Apart from oppressive foreign rule, and the desire to escape from a society in which corruption was rampant and life uncertain, the phenomenon of monasticism owed something to the widespread belief that the end of the world and the Second Coming were at hand.

Those were indeed violent and unsettled times. In 616 the Egyptians were temporarily freed from the Byzantine yoke when a Persian army under Chosroes invaded the country, but a dozen years later Emperor Heraclitus re-established Byzantine control and attempted to restore law and order to the chaotic land. Under Cyrus, the Greek Patriarch of Alexandria and Governor of Egypt, harsh persecution of the Monophysite Copts, in a vain attempt to re-instate Orthodoxy, was renewed in 632. Not surprisingly, after six years of terror, the Egyptian population welcomed the invading Arabs or at most proffered weak resistance.

Arab Egypt

The Conquest

For the militant Arab caliphate, intent on conquering the world for Islam, Egypt was an attractive and easy target. Not only was it a rich source of revenue and food, but it was also the stepping stone for the conquest of the whole of North Africa. With the Byzantine government and forces in disarray and a downtrodden, passive population, there seemed little likelihood of much resistance. And so it proved.

In 639, an army of 4,000 horsemen under Amr Ibn el-As, the general of Caliph Omar, reached Egypt overland, thus avoiding the Byzantine fleet, to be followed the next year by a further 12,000 men. In November 641, Patriarch Cyrus as governor of Egypt negotiated a treaty whereby Alexandria would be surrendered to Amr the following September. In the meantime, the Arab general founded the settlement of Fustat, near modern Cairo, as his base. According to the terms of the treaty, in return for paying a tribute and supplying the occupying troops with food, the Christian inhabitants were to be left free to practise their religion and administer their affairs. Many Egyptians regarded the Byzantine defeat as divine retribution for the persecution they had suffered under Patriarch Cyrus, now replaced by the Coptic (Monophysite) Patriarch Benjamin who had previously been ejected by Emperor Heraclitus. With their church hierarchy restored and administration in their own hands, the Copts had every reason to be pleased with the new dispensation, particularly as they believed that the Bedouins would soon return to the desert with their tribute and plunder. They could not have been more mistaken.

Islamic rule was here to stay. The Muslim religion was still less than a century old, but was rapidly establishing itself as a major faith. Since in Islam there is no real separation between religion and politics, any country that comes under its rule will be fundamentally influenced in its outlook, and in legal, moral and social practices, according to the dictates of the Islamic code. It will also become part of the community of Islam. Although Egypt retained its individuality, from that time onwards it became a member of the 'Islamic family', a group of nations expected to acknowledge their common cause in upholding the religion of the Prophet.

At first Damascus was the recognized centre of the Islamic world; it was succeeded in about 750 by Baghdad, and later, as we shall see, by Egypt. Not all the Egyptians immediately adopted the new faith. On the contrary, the vast majority remained Christians until at least a hundred years after the conquest, though certain factors helped to speed the process of conversion along. One was the imposition of a tax upon any citizen not practising Islam, while another was the growing incidence of intermarriage between Arabs and Christians. During the first century of Islamic rule, there was a general wave of Arab immigration into Egypt, initially concentrated in the eastern Delta region known as the Hawf. Most immigrants were warriors, who were not at first allowed to own land, for fear that this would lessen their enthusiasm for war. Intermarriage with Christian women was a way around the prohibition, and a practice which steadily increased the Muslim proportion of the population.

The term 'Arab' was at first used for those of pure Arabian blood, with Islamic converts of other nationalities being known as mawalis or 'clients'. However, as time went on, this distinction became eroded both by intermarriage, as in Egypt, and by the teachings of the Koran itself, which preached equality of the faithful. This led to the use of the term 'Arabic' to apply to all who partook in Islamic faith and culture. Use of the Arab language was also integral to Islam, and thus in Egypt Arabic had replaced

Greek as the official language by 710. Coptic was still the tongue of the people at that time, but its use slowly diminished, eventually dying out as a spoken language in the seventeenth century; today it is found only in the liturgy of the Coptic Christian Church. To all intents and purposes Egypt was now a fully-fledged Islamic nation.

The Coming of the Turks

Progress was not entirely smooth. Taxation imposed on the country by its government grew heavier and heavier, provoking rebellion among the people. This eventually weakened the rule of the original dynasty of Arab caliphs, but any hopes of re-establishing a permanent independence from foreign rule were dashed by the arrival of new Turkish governors. Turkish soldiers, some of whom had previously held office as praetorian guards in Baghdad, began to replace Arab warriors in about 850, and in 868 a new Turkish dynasty was founded under Sultan Tulun. Their policy of taxation was no lighter than that of their predecessors, and their discrimination against Christians so much more severe that the native population converted overwhelmingly to Islam at this time.

Turkish rule of Egypt passed through many phases, but lasted in all for nearly a thousand years. A succession of autocratic, but fairly benevolent despots, including some of Kurdish or Circassian origin, helped to give Egypt a new stability. At the high point of their reign, following the destruction of Baghdad by the Mongols in the thirteenth century, Egypt became the centre of Islamic culture, and the stronghold of Islamic faith against Christian attack. From being a mere outpost of Islam it had become its bastion at a time of significant political, literary and religious development throughout the 'civilized' world.

Ibn Tulun, the first Turkish caliph, brought general prosperity and stability to Egypt, founding a dynasty that ruled from 868 to 904. He began a successful construction programme, and left his permanent mark in the form of the great mosque in Cairo that bears his name. Legend has it that Tulun was idly twisting a piece of paper around his finger, when he suddenly had a vision of its pleasing, spiralling shape becoming the minaret for his new mosque, the groundplan of which is said to be based on the Kaaba, the holy shrine at Mecca.

The Tulun Dynasty was followed by an unsettled, rebellious period of about thirty years, after which the next dynasty was established by Mohammed Tughi, known better as Ikhshid, who is remembered in particular for his agricultural reforms and for the blossoming of the arts that occurred during his reign. A later ruler of the same dynasty, however, is recalled with less affection: the name of the Abyssinian eunuch Kafur became synonymous with the word for tyranny in the Arab world, although his supposed reign of terror has never been confirmed by historians. Following his death, strong rule was once again succeeded by weak government, exacerbated by low floods and bad harvests. Economic uncertainty and low morale made it relatively easy for General Jawhar, of the Fatimid caliphate, to gain control in 969.

The Fatimids

Egyptian Islamic civilization was still developing, and the two hundred years of Fatimid rule formed one of the most brilliant periods of its culture. The Fatimids, who took their name from the daughter of the Prophet Mohammed, were the minority Shi'ite sect. As such, they were regarded as heretics by the orthodox Sunnis who ruled in Baghdad. Fatimid religion took a bizarre turn, however, in 1018 when Caliph Hakim became insane and declared himself to be God. This eventually led to the founding of a new sect, the Druzes, who believed that Hakim was not dead but had temporarily vanished, soon to return in Messianic glory.

When the Fatimids seized power over Egypt in 969, their military leader, General Gohar, set up a new caliph's residence north of el-Katabi, the Tulunid quarter of what is now Cairo, and is thus considered the real founder of the city. It is said that as he laid the first stone, the planet Mars, known in Arabic as *el-Qahira*, 'the victorious', appeared in the sky — hence the name Cairo.

The position of Cairo had long been a favoured one because the Nile could easily be crossed at this point, thanks to the islands of el-Gazira and el-Rawda. The earliest recorded settlement there was known as Kheri-aha, 'the place of combat', supposedly the site of a battle between Seth and Horus. The Greeks later renamed it Babylon — their interpretation of the ancient Egyptian name Per-Hapi-en-On ('Nile house of Heliopolis'). At the time of the Arab conquest, General Amr Ibn el-As founded his camp at el-Fustat (now the old quarter of Cairo), which developed into the new capital of Egypt. This was expanded northward by the Tulunids, but it was under the Fatimids that the city emerged as a major centre of learning and religious culture. The el-Azhar mosque was completed by Gohar in 972, and in 988 the Islamic university was founded. A later ruler, el-Mustansir, added to Egypt's reputation as a civilized nation by acquiring a library of over 100,000 books.

The Fatimids were eventually overthrown by their own bodyguards, who had been gaining ascendancy along with the military officers and mercenaries. One factor was the decline in official tolerance of ethnic and religious minorities. Angered by this, the exotic mixture of nationalities in the armed forces also helped foment the uprising against the ruling dynasty, who were after all themselves foreigners in Egypt.

Saladin

It was now time for Kurds to rule Egypt: the Ayyubid Dynasty founded by the celebrated Saladin (Salah el–Din, 1171-1193), famed for his role in the Crusades and still regarded as a hero today. In 1187 he captured Jerusalem, a venture which the Fatimids had quickly abandoned after one hopeless attempt. Previously chief minister of the sultan he helped to overthrow, the new ruler began the construction of Cairo's immense Citadel, for centuries one of the greatest fortresses of the Islamic world. Built partly of stone from some of the smaller pyramids, it took thirty years to complete. In order to strengthen his position against the Crusaders, Saladin extended his military power over Syria and Mesopotamia, a power sustained by Kurds of his own race and by Mamluk slave guards from Turkey.

But the glorious flowering of the arts and scholarship, the magnificent new buildings, were enjoyed only by those living in the sophisticated areas of Egypt, namely Cairo and Alexandria. Elsewhere, the vast majority of country dwellers lived in abject poverty, their welfare of little concern to the governing elite. By ignoring the state of the populace, and concentrating on foreign expansion, the Holy War, and furthering their own ethnic interests, the Ayyubids made themselves vulnerable, like their predecessors. After a comparatively short period in power, some seventy years, they were ousted by the military forces they had maintained for their own protection.

The Mamluks

The Mamluks were members of a caste of slaves brought over from Turkey, an ethnically mixed group of Turks, Kurds, South Slavs, Albanians, Mongols and other central Asian tribes. Their slavery continued when they were brought to Egypt as soldiers: the very word 'Mamluk' (Mameluke) means 'owned'. Their status was unusual, however, in that they were not so much owned by as 'bonded' to their masters. This bond, or kinship, meant that a Mamluk slave would often take his master's position of authority after his death. When the Mamluks wrested the entire control of Egypt from their collective masters, they kept their military outlook, forming a hierarchical warrior caste, and always living apart from the native people.

Though always soldiers at heart, they were not barbarians, and under their rule Egyptian culture continued to flourish, with new minarets thrusting up towards heaven like the cathedral spires of their Gothic counterparts in Europe. Official patronage of the arts and learning stimulated the production of illuminated manuscripts and the crafting of exquisite work in ivory, metal, clay, glass and leather. The great flowering of the Middle Ages in Europe was well matched in the cities of Egypt, by then the dominant power in the Arab world. Much of the money poured into the arts was gained from trade, and such commercial success also helped to fund public works, such as civil engineering schemes designed to improve the nation's economy. Any such schemes in Egypt usually involve the water of the Nile, its life blood, and now new irrigation canals, bridges, dams and aqueducts helped men to use this precious resource more effectively.

More unusually, a postal system was introduced by one of the first and most famous Mamluk sultans, Baibars (1260-1277), although this was designed to promote military efficiency rather than commerce or private letter-writing. The Mamluks appear to have been shrewd administrators, since they were said to favour employing Copts in official posts above their Islamic compatriots because of their sound business sense and accounting skills.

The Mamluk era is generally divided into two periods, the first known as Bahri or Turkish rule, which ran from 1250 to 1382, and the second as Buryi (Circassian), which lasted until 1517, when Egypt was incorporated in the Ottoman empire. Although this marked the end of their absolute rule, yet Mamluk influence persisted until the early nineteenth century, when it was finally destroyed by Mehmet Ali.

Under the Mamluks, Egypt came to exert control over an area extending from the mountains of southern Turkey in the north to Nubia in the south, and from the Mediterranean to the Arabian Sea. In 1260, the Mamluks proved their fighting skills by driving back the Mongols in Palestine, thus averting the imminent threat of a Mongol invasion of Egypt. Following this, Sultan Baibars conducted many successful campaigns against the Crusaders, the Armenians and the Seljuk Turks of Asia Minor.

The Ottoman Empire

But eventually even the Mamluks' military prowess failed them. Economic disasters, internal squabbles and the grandiose notions of an ageing leader, Qansuh, finally weakened them to the point where they could no longer withstand foreign invasion. They were no match in battle for the new ruler of the Ottoman empire, Selim I, and his well-trained forces. After defeating the Mamluks in a battle near Aleppo fought in 1516, Selim

59. The minarets of a mosque appear to emerge out of the ruins of the temple of Amenophis III at Luxor. In the foreground are the slender columns of Roman and Byzantine buildings.

60. Valley of the Kings, relief of Horus above the entrance to the tomb of Sety I. Its painted reliefs, among the finest in ancient Egyptian art, compare well with those of the temple at Abydos founded by the same ruler.

62. Thebes, entrance to the tomb of Sety (Sethos) I, who died in about 1279 B.C. One of the most beautiful and best preserved of all the tombs in the Valley of the Kings, it was raided in 1817 by Giovanni Battista Belzoni, who sold the lovely alabaster sarcophagus in London, where it is now in the Soane Museum.

61. Dendera, a view of the temple and its sacred precinct, looking towards the Nile, which here takes its great sweep. The temple, dedicated to the mother goddess Hathor, is among the best preserved and most recent, dating from ptolemaic and Roman times, though this had been a cult site since the Old Kingdom.

63. Keeping God's House clean. An unofficial guide awaits visitors outside the Ramesseum at Thebes West. The Greeks called this temple the Memnonium or Tomb of User-maetre, one of the many names of Ramesses II. Its precinct, enclosed by a mud-brick wall 10 ft thick, also contains a huge number of storerooms. (pp. 110-111)

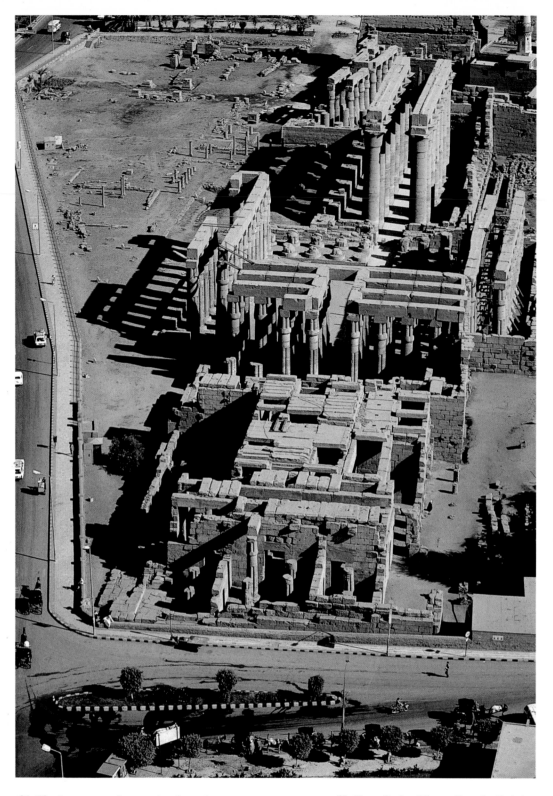

64. The Luxor temple complex from the south-west. In the foreground is the sanctuary of Alexander the Great, beyond it the courtyard, and then the colonnade of Amenophis III. The dusty, dull look of the masonry takes on a magical glow when the 'son et lumière' spectacle is held here.

65. Kom Ombo. The well and adjoining cistern with a staircase leading into it constituted a hydraulic device connected with the cult and rituals of Sobek, the crocodile god. The temple here was dedicated to Sobek and Horus, the falcon god.

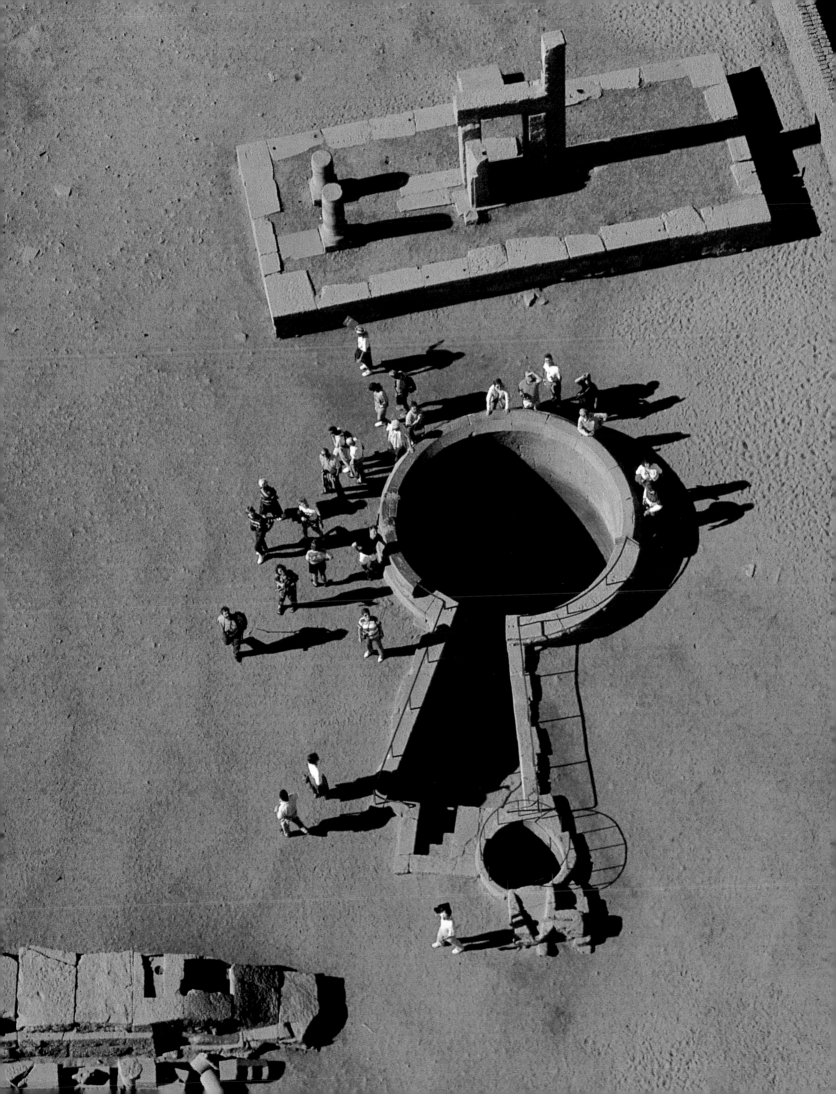

66. *Karnak in the setting sun. Its last rays penetrate through the mighty gate into the innermost sanctuaries of the Great House of Amon.*

67. *Luxor, two of four seated statues of Ramesses II. The Luxor temple, the supreme achievement of Eighteenth-Dynasty architecture, was built by Amenophis III as a gift to his 'father', Amon-Ra, the God of Gods. Under Akhenaten, his 'heretic' son, everything here connected with Amon was defaced, but the reliefs were restored by later rulers.*

68. Thebes West, the second pylon of the Ramesseum with four beheaded statues of Ramesses II. It was here that Shelley, seeing the shattered remains of a colossal granite figure of the King, was inspired to write the famous lines:
'My name is Ozymandias, King of Kings: Look on my works, ye mighty, and despair.'

69. Karnak, the great courtyard of the temple of Amon. This papyrus bundle column is the sole survivor of ten that were part of the colonnaded hall built by Taharqa, an Ethiopian pharaoh of the Twenty-fifth Dynasty.

70. Karnak. A palm stands as Nature's counterpart to the obelisk of Queen Hatshepsut. The eastern part of the Karnak complex beyond the fourth and fifth pylons, is not as impressive and well preserved as the western, but the structures are extremely intricate and have fine reliefs on the walls.

71. Kom Ombo, stone flower capitals of the temple of Sobek and Horus, typical of the ptolemaic period. The reliefs on the walls show Ptolemy VI, VII and VIII with Cleopatra II and III offering to the temple's deities.

72. The southern of the two Colossi of
Memnon. In the earthquake of 27 B.C. his
companion fell and cracked. This damage
was said to be the cause of the humming
noise which the statue produced every
morning at sunrise. It is reported that
restoration work carried out by Emperor
Septimius Severus in A.D. 200 silenced the
Colossus.

73. Thebes West, the Colossi of Memnon. Called 'the two idols' by the locals, they both represent Pharaoh Amenophis III and stood in front of his now vanished mortuary temple. Carved from single blocks of sandstone, they were originally at least 64 ft high.

74. Luxor, the avenue of sphinxes added to the temple by Pharaoh Nectanebo I of the Thirtieth Dynasty, the last ruler to alter the temple, built by Amenophis III of the Eighteenth Dynasty.

75. Karnak, one of the avenues of sphinxes along which the annual procession of the festival of Amon progressed from the Nile to the Great Temple. The procession, which arrived from Luxor by boat, is repeatedly represented in the reliefs of the huge complex.

76. The island of Agilka (Agilqiya), the new home of most of the monuments originally raised on the fabulous island of Philae, which was subject to flooding after the building of the Old Dam at Aswan, and more seriously threatened by the High Dam. UNESCO rescuers moved the monuments stone by stone, then reassembled them on the higher nearby island.

77. The core of the great pyramid of el-Lahun in the Fayyum, more correctly called the pyramid complex of Senusert (Senwosret) II of the Twelfth Dynasty.

78. The collapsed pyramid of Meidum, probably begun by King Huni of the Third Dynasty and completed by his son, Snofru.

79. Saqqara. A camel ride will take the visitor around the great stepped pyramid of Pharaoh Zoser. The Saqqara complex was built by Imhotep, the Pharaoh's architect, between 2667 and 2648 B.C.

80. Edfu, the temple of Horus, among the best preserved of all ancient Egyptian temples. It was begun as late as 237 B.C. under Ptolemy III. Until the mid-nineteenth century, the temple lay buried under the dwellings of the town, with only the lofty pylon rising above the roofs.

took control of Egypt the following year, having already subdued Persia and Syria in the first five years of his reign. With this conquest, Egypt lost its independent status and became a province of the Ottoman empire.

Now Istanbul was the Islamic centre to which Egypt was forced to turn for religious and political guidance. Selim had been honoured with the keys of the Holy City of Islam, and the standard and the cloak of the Prophet were now lodged in Istanbul as tokens of his role as 'Protector of the Holy Places'. Rather than being strengthened through association with the Turkish empire, though, Egypt went into a period of progressive decline. It was ruled by a governor or pasha, appointed by the sultan, in collaboration with a council ('divan') of twenty-four Mamluk beys, responsible for collecting taxes. The pashas were no more concerned about the condition of the peasant in the fields than their predecessors. Although they paid some attention to improving agricultural methods, and even eased the tax that the *fellahin* had to pay, any benefits were quickly offset by the greed of a fast-growing land-owning class of oppressors — the Mamluks once again. Displaced from their position of supreme authority, they turned their attention to establishing their rights over local territory. Before long they became so powerful in this capacity that they were, in effect, joint rulers of Egypt with the Ottomans in an unstable and constant struggle for supremacy. As the empire weakened, so did the pasha's authority. Real power was in the hands of the two principle Mamluk leaders, bearing the titles Sheik el–Balad and Emir el–Hajj, who were often in conflict.

European Invasion

In 1768 came the first real move to break away from the Ottoman empire. When Ali Bey became Sheik el–Balad, he ceased to pay tribute to Turkey, coined his own money, and joined forces with the Russians in the Russo-Turkish War. This attempt to assert independence died with Ali Bey, who succumbed to wounds after a battle against the forces of his ambitious son-in-law, Abu Dahab. The latter, on becoming Sheik el–Balad, again recognized the Porte's supremacy, but this was to last only thirty years more, until the French invaded Egypt with Napoleon at their head. Egypt was already showing an interest in being drawn back into European affairs, and in fact had become a victim of its own machinations, by signing trade treaties with both Britain and France to exploit the rivalry between them.

The attempt to inflame this rivalry was successful, but the result not what the Egyptians had anticipated. It motivated Napoleon Bonaparte to invade, directing his army towards fertile Egypt, a country strategically placed between Africa and Asia, and a prize for any ambitious European nation. From a military point of view, Egypt was in a weak position, its population reduced to three or four million, little more than half the number at the time of the Arab conquest. It was not a united country; the split between the ruling military aristocracy and the rest of the population had existed for centuries, and a further division was now opened up between the ruling factions of Ottomans and Mamluks. Napoleon had little trouble in defeating the Mamluk army at the Battle of the Pyramids in 1798, and established control of Egypt shortly afterwards.

Bonaparte's triumph was not entirely unwelcome to the populace, though he failed to convince the sheiks in his placatory opening speeches that he was a disciple of Mohammed, guided and protected by the Prophet himself. Egypt's connection with the Ottoman empire was now severed, the power of the Mamluks largely eroded (temporarily, as it turned out), and new possibilities of equality sprang up to delight its citizens. Although the secular, rational approach of Napoleonic rule was deeply disturbing to their faith, it nevertheless offered chances of improved conditions and opportunities for self-government. France would represent the ultimate control over Egypt, but self-government in most matters would be encouraged under the leadership of the Divan, or Administrative Council.

Napoleon brought with him to Egypt a group of 165 cultured gentlemen, experts in the fields of science, literature and the arts. These were to form the vanguard of a new assembly whose purpose would be to study Egyptian life — to research its history and resources, to set up printing presses and academies, and to produce innovative plans for its development. This learned circle became known as the Institute of Egypt, and even though French rule in Egypt proved to be very brief, its influence was profound, paving the way for later projects. The interest of its members in the ancient history and archaeology of Egypt marks the founding of Egyptology as a study in its own right.

Much remained at the planning stage, but some practical advances were made by the French, including the publication of two journals covering political and economic matters, and, of more lasting importance, of a twenty-volume survey of contemporary Egypt entitled *Description de l'Egypte*. Experimental chemistry and physics laboratories were set up, and the Egyptians were treated to the novelty of watching a balloon launch from one of the city squares in Cairo.

But Bonaparte's fortunes were precarious; the Ottoman Sultan had formed an alliance with both Britain and Russia. It inflicted a crushing defeat upon the French fleet in Abukir Bay and upon the army which had advanced into Syria to defend Egypt from Turkish invasion. Bonaparte himself retreated to Paris in 1799, leaving behind deputies who struggled on for another two years before the tottering French regime finally crumbled.

Mehmet Ali

For a further two years, Egypt was in a state of upheaval almost bordering on civil war. The Mamluks and the Ottomans were still at each other's throats, but neither side was strong enough to take control. Finally, a leader emerged who had both the pragmatism and the statesmanship to turn Egypt back into a united nation. This was Mohammed or Mehmet Ali, an illiterate Albanian merchant-turned-soldier, whose abilities raised him from lowly origins to become one of the greatest Egyptian politicians of all time. His dynastic line survived through various vicissitudes until 1952, and because his rule had such a deep effect upon the course of Egyptian history, it is worth describing it in some detail.

During Mehmet Ali's rule, from 1805 to 1847, political, administrative, technological and agricultural reforms transformed the life of the country. He himself was less interested in social reform and justice than in making Egypt strong and profitable. A dual career in the army and in trade reflected his two abiding interests, in military strategy and in commerce. These were the aims he pursued, and they could only be achieved by changing a social order whose corruption and backwardness were in themselves a barrier to progress. As a soldier, Mehmet Ali had first-hand experience of both British and French troops, which opened his eyes to the advantages of European technology, something he now intended to import into Egypt.

His power was formally granted by the Ottoman Sultan, but in effect he made Egypt self-governing. The Ottoman empire, later known as 'The Sick Man of Europe', was hardly a strong enough edifice to support an Egypt that was now ambitious to prosper and grow. To create a strong and independent state, Mehmet Ali first had to attend to internal politics and achieve a degree of unity among its people. He set about eradicating the last traces of Mamluk power, using the squabbles among their leaders to loosen their hold on the country. He also managed to turn the general population against both the Mamluks and the Ottomans by laying the blame for all Egypt's ills at their door. Bloody means were also used; in the most famous incident of all, he invited nearly five hundred Mamluk leaders to a banquet in the Cairo Citadel and there had them all massacred.

One of Mehmet Ali's most significant reforms concerned land ownership, long overdue for radical change. For centuries, lazy rulers had parcelled out gifts of land to the military aristocracy, impoverishing the native population and ultimately weakening their own position by creating an armed, ambitious, land-owning class, the beys. In later times, land was granted in return for tax-collecting responsibilities, a system known as *iltizam*, which undermined central control and left the *fellahin* at the mercy of the landowners, who avidly stripped the assets and produce of their territory.

Mehmet Ali's campaign included a sweeping policy of land nationalization. By reclaiming land from the Mamluks, some of the main benefactors from the *iltizam* system, he had found another means of reducing their power. But although he redistributed land among the peasants and the village headmen, this ultimately led to a new class of wealthy landowners, and to the growth of large country estates. He also made tax-free gifts of land to his own state officials, and to other officials and regional governors in return for tax-collecting duties. Life tenure of land eventually evolved into hereditary ownership, so that although the old stranglehold on land ownership and use had been broken, the new pattern itself created a wealthy minority who controlled the land, albeit with better cultivation methods and without the extreme oppression of the *fellahin* that had existed before.

Mehmet Ali also turned his attention to the sorry state of the Egyptian troops. The existing forces were too wayward and indeed dangerous to bring back under control, so he looked to other sources of fighting men to serve the new nation. The native peasants, the *fellahin*, had never been called upon to fight — one advantage, at least, of the old regime, was that the military aristocracy had fought all the battles. He tried to avoid turning to

Edward Lane: Sketch in a guest chamber.

131

the general population, who were in any case needed to revive the economy, but after an unsuccessful recruitment experiment, during which thousands of imported Sudanese died of disease, he was forced to call upon his own people to fill the ranks. Training was now carried out at professional military schools and colleges, initiating the new army into strategies of modern warfare. The first such college was sited at Aswan, far enough away from Cairo to prevent serious trouble if the cadets should decide to mutiny.

In order to provide a high enough standard among army recruits, general education was also improved, and schools were founded upon European lines. Mehmet Ali was in his forties before he learnt to read, but like many people who have missed the chance of a good education themselves, he appreciated its value. He sent hundreds of young Egyptians to study in Paris and London, so that they were able to return to their country with an up-to-date training in agriculture, engineering, medicine and industry. Hospitals were now set up, and though this new interest in medicine was also chiefly intended to benefit the army, its effects upon the general health care of the populace were far-reaching.

Side by side with these reforms, industrial innovations were under way, giving Egypt a new and welcome financial security. Cotton production, now state-controlled, was developed to become the economic mainstay of the nation, its revenue useful for funding the military manoeuvres in which the Pasha liked to indulge. Other factories and arsenals were also built, manufacturing goods such as paper, sugar, chemicals, weapons and army uniforms. Although machinery and technology were still crude compared with the best that could be found in Europe, they nevertheless proved a major advance in Egypt. Road and water transport was also improved so that distribution of these products could be carried out more efficiently. New dams, canals and irrigation systems were built with the help of French engineers, which allowed a million more acres of land to be brought into cultivation.

The nation remained firmly Muslim in religion and outlook, and Turkish was retained as the official language until 1845, when Arabic began to take its place. (Mehmet Ali himself never learnt to speak Arabic.) But, increasingly, Egypt looked to Europe for guidance; Europeans held office in Mehmet Ali's government, and elements of the French legal system were introduced alongside the Islamic code of law. The communication between Egypt and Europe became two way, as a wave of foreign immigration began to wash into Egypt, bringing workers of all classes from France, Italy and Greece.

Mehmet Ali's foreign policy remained aggressive. His Middle Eastern military campaigns were helped by the expertise of his oldest son, Ibrahim, and sometimes hindered by its lack in his second son, Tussun. During his reign he conquered the Sudan and found favour with the Ottoman Sultan by fighting off an invasion of the holy Islamic land. His European sympathies did not extend to Britain, for he suspected that any British interest in Egypt would prove a threat to his own government.

This fear was well-founded, for ultimately the British became deeply concerned by Mehmet Ali's occupation of lands all along the eastern coast of the Red Sea. Finally, Britain, France, Prussia, Austria and Russia formed an alliance in 1840 to curtail his ambitions, and using armed force, stripped him of all his conquests except the Sudan. By this time, Mehmet Ali was an old man and in 1847 was ready to abdicate in favour of his son, his position as hereditary pasha having been 'confirmed' by the alliance. Ibrahim, however, died within a year, and his nephew Abbas, son of Tussun, proved a dour and reactionary successor.

The Making of the Modern State

The Khedive and the Canal

The era of Mehmet Ali marked the transition into what we would call the modern world. Although his immediate successors made little impact, Ismail, another of his grandsons, was in a different league. He took office in 1863 and was later granted the title of khedive, a term meaning viceroy, and carrying with it the rights of direct succession for his own heirs. He inherited a country which was fast declining into chaos, one which aped European sophistication yet lacked the efficient infrastructure to support such ambition.

But soon one factor irrevocably changed the face of Egypt, and permanently affected its relationships with foreign powers. This was the opening of the Suez Canal in 1869. Even in ancient Egypt there had been dreams of such a waterway to link the Mediterranean with the Red Sea. In recent years it had been considered too difficult to create because it was believed that the level of the Red Sea was about twenty feet above sea level. Napoleon's own engineers had told him that such a project was out of the question. However, in the 1830s a British engineer proved that the levels were not incompatible, and in 1859 work had begun on the canal under the guidance of a French engineer, Ferdinand de Lesseps. Not all outside powers shared this jubilation; Britain, for one, was apprehensive, foreseeing that control of the canal would become a key issue in world affairs.

For the time being, Ismail courted the whole of Europe. The completion of the canal gave him the excuse to invite foreign heads of state to the official opening, an extravagant affair mounted at enormous cost to the nation. Determined to take Egypt further down the road to modernization, European-style, he offered important posts in government and in education to eminent Europeans. He wanted his country to rank with the great Western powers, and to put Cairo on a par with London, Paris and Rome. He also desired a substantial African empire, such as Britain and France now had, and he even hoped one day to lead the Ottoman empire itself. 'My country,' he said, 'no longer belongs to Africa; it is part of Europe.'

It seems extraordinary that during centuries of Ottoman rule, no Turkish sultan had ever visited Egypt. With an eye to improving his chances, Ismail invited the current sultan, who arrived in 1863 and was received with lavish hospitality. Such a ploy may have been obvious, but it worked. In May 1866 Sultan Abdel decreed Ismail to be his appointed successor.

In one sense, Ismail was attempting to run with the hare and hunt with the hounds by courting favour both with the major European powers and the Sultan. He was profligate with money; the opening of the Suez Canal, beneficial as it may have been in general terms, brought the country near to bankruptcy, and the amounts that Ismail had to borrow from abroad to shore up his finances led to unwelcome European interference in Egyptian affairs. Now Ismail's financial entanglements began to cause alarm in the Turkish court; the Sultan reacted by revoking Egypt's rights to independence, and decreed that no more money was to be borrowed from Europe.

Ismail was not deterred, however, and concentrated on cultivating his relationship with France. But when France was defeated in the Franco-Prussian War of 1870–71, his hopes of success in that quarter were crushed, and he resorted to patching up his quarrel with the Sultan. In this, at least, he succeeded, and by 1873 had regained all his rights from the ruler, obtaining what was known as an Imperial Rescript, which entitled him to rule and raise money independently. And, with France no longer a useful ally, he turned to Britain for support.

The British Lion insures its key to India: Disraeli buying shares in the Suez Canal from the Khedive Ismail. (Punch magazine, 1876)

British Intervention

Britain had hitherto not looked favourably upon the Khedive, who had sided with its old rival, France, and used French money and expertise to build the Suez Canal. But Ismail's overtures were finally met with an offer to buy 44 per cent of the shares in the Suez Canal Company, for which the British government would give four million pounds. Prime Minister Disraeli arranged for the money to be paid from a loan made by the House of Rothschild, but Gladstone, leading the Liberal opposition, violently opposed the deal, believing it both foolish and dangerous to entangle Britain in Egyptian affairs.

The British had paid a comparatively modest sum for the shares, not enough to save Egypt's fortunes. A formal declaration of bankruptcy was made in April 1876. Although revenue in Egypt was up, from five million pounds sterling annually in 1864, to around 150 million by 1875, and although exports also tripled in this time, Ismail's spending habits had taken the economy into dramatic decline.

In order to save its shareholding, Britain was forced into further negotiations, with the upshot that both Britain and France now took joint control of Egypt's financial affairs, each installing a controller-general there, and instituting a repayment scheme which would cost Egypt two thirds of its annual revenue. The controllers-general also ordered an enquiry into Ismail's own financial management, which concluded that the Khedive must hand over much of his authority to ministers with more sense and expertise than he himself possessed.

British standards prevailed; Ismail was forced to sign an agreement outlawing the slave trade. His grandfather, Mehmet Ali, had brought back thousands of black African slaves with whom he hoped to create an entire

Ismailia, named after the Khedive Ismail, was founded as the administrative headquarters for the construction of the Suez Canal.

134

army, but was thwarted in this ambition by the slaves' unfortunate habit of dying when transplanted into a different environment. Ismail's own dreams of African conquest were, in a way, realized, for the British began a series of military campaigns against black Africa, using Egypt as a base, and involving the Khedive's troops in triumphant expeditions into the areas of the great lakes, the Congo basin, and Ethiopia.

Despite financial disasters, Ismail's reign of some sixteen years also saw many advances. Irrigation and cultivation were improved, and Egypt had now entered the foreign trade markets, using cash crops of sugar and cotton to boost exports. Banking standards were raised to a European level, with the Bank of Egypt becoming the Anglo-Egyptian Bank and other major European banks establishing branches in Egypt, linking it to the international money market. And although the Suez Canal was the crowning glory of the age, 112 other canals were also dug, among them the longest of all, the Ibrahimiya Canal. Ismail also built 400 bridges across the Nile, the most famous being the Kasr el-Nil in Cairo. Communications in general were improved; railways and telegraph lines were extended, and a proper national postal service was instituted.

Ismail also played his part in supporting new cultural institutions; during his reign the Geographical Society, the National Library, and the Observatory were all established. From the 1870s onwards there was a great flowering of artistic activity, inspired, perhaps, by European culture, which was now popular in the theatres and in the Opera House at Cairo, but also bringing increased appreciation of Egypt's own musical and literary traditions. Foreign imports, it seemed, had helped Egypt to become more aware of its own heritage.

The country was still under foreign control, however, and its government by no means secure. With Ismail's army turned against him, he was therefore strongly advised to abdicate in favour of his son Tawfiq. France, Britain and now Germany and Austria too (who had financial interests at stake) pressured him into making this move in 1879. But the situation was still highly unstable, with different factions proclaiming themselves as pro-Ottoman, pro-European, pro-Khedive, and even pro-Orabist, a new nationalist military movement led by Colonel Orabi Pasha. Tawfiq's rule could not last long.

British Rule

By 1881 the army was in the ascendancy, and in 1882 Tawfiq fled into exile. The Orabist army troops headed a struggle for liberation with the rallying call 'Egypt to the Egyptians'. With the financial backing they had gained from industrialists and landowners, they might indeed have won had not the British Navy been lying in wait off the Alexandrian coast, ready to suppress any uprising.

The subsequent battle took its toll on the port of Alexandria, and the British forces moved further into Egypt, using the Nile and the Suez Canal as corridors of invasion. They reinstated the Khedive, and declared Orabi himself to be a traitor. He retaliated by declaring the Khedive a traitor to both Egypt and Allah. But power was now in the hands of the British, and as they advanced, so the rebel army collapsed, a bitter disappointment for the nationalists. By September 1882, Cairo had fallen, and Egypt was under British rule.

The whole world was stirred by this turn of events. Britain's avowed aim was to remain in occupation only for as long as it took to restore order. Whether or not this was sincerely meant is open to debate, but certainly, as it turned out, British involvement in Egyptian affairs was far from short-lived. Not until 1922 did Britain formally recognize Egypt's independence, and not until after the Suez affair in 1956 did the last British troops leave the country.

At the time of the invasion, Lord Grenville, British Foreign Secretary, issued the following statement of intent:

' Although for the present a British force remains in Egypt for the preservation of public tranquility, HM Government are desirous of withdrawing it as soon as the state of the country, and the organization of proper means for the maintenance of the Khedive's authority will admit it. In the meanwhile, the position in which HM Government are placed towards His Highness imposes upon them the duty of giving advice with the object of securing that the order of things to be established shall be of satisfactory character, and possess the elements of stability and progress.'

Lord Dufferin, sent by HM Government to Egypt as a special envoy to investigate the problem, was doubtful whether an early withdrawal would be possible, claiming that a hasty removal could be 'fatal to the prosperity and good administration of the country'. He was instructed, nevertheless, to 'draw up a scheme for the restoration of the country, which would conform to a policy of withdrawing the British garrison at an early date.' Dufferin's report on the reorganization of the Egyptian government was submitted in February 1883, leading to the appointment of Lord Cromer as British Agent and Consul-General. In Parliament that year, Queen Victoria confidently told the nation that withdrawal of British troops was 'proceeding as expeditiously as a prudent consideration of the circumstances will permit.'

Her confidence was shaken, however, by a new disaster which threatened Egypt's borders. The popular and eccentric figure of General Gordon was killed in the Sudan, a victim of the Mahdi rebel forces who had taken control from the remnants of Mehmet Ali's old government there. Gordon, no stranger to the area, was ordered to assist the evacuation of the Egyptian garrisons as quickly as possible. But he stayed on, hoping to turn the tide of events, and died of a spear wound as Khartoum finally fell to the rebels.

Thus the temporary occupation of Egypt extended indefinitely. The British had landed themselves in a situation in which they were unpopular, but from which they could not easily withdraw. Lord Cromer remained in office for some twenty-four years, during which time two khedives came and went, sovereigns more in name than reality. Cromer used his time diligently to set Egyptian finances in order, balancing the books as Ismail had failed so dismally to do. He also created a Civil Service in which native Egyptians were included, based on the model used in India, where he had previously served.

Cromer, known as 'el–Lurd' to the Egyptians, established a healthy economic climate, introduced much-needed reforms in administration and education, and carried out a programme of land reclamation and irrigation. There were certainly benefits to many sections of Egyptian society under British rule; the *fellahin* were redeemed from the worst of the oppression which they had suffered under generations of oriental tyranny. But the population still lacked self-determination, and advances in education were confined to a privileged minority. In time this fomented enough national fervour to create a serious threat to foreign rule.

A new nationalist faction was formed by Mustafa Kamel, a young French-educated lawyer of strong Islamic beliefs. Its early success was short-lived and Kamel's untimely death in 1908 brought it to a close. But by

86. A neat Muslim cemetery on the fringe of
the desert, where there is plenty of room for
the houses of the dead.

87. *A camel market in Upper Egypt. One of the longest trade routes of Egypt runs across the desert from Asyut to the Sudan. Camels are still the best means of transport for long journeys across such terrain. On the way to Abu Simbel, the traveller will often see camel caravans slowly making their way across the endless Nubian Desert.*

88,90. *A Nubian village on the Nile near Aswan in Upper Egypt. The Muslim cemetery with a mosque on its sandy outskirts has some more imposing tombs, domed or conical, where persons of greater wealth or importance were buried.*

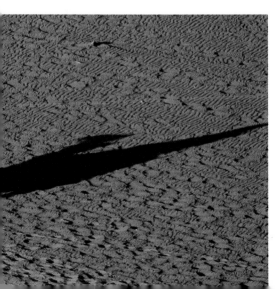

*89. Long shadows on the Nubian Desert.
Slowly but surely the camel drivers follow
the desert track alongside Lake Nasser.*

91. Thebes West, the house of a pilgrim to Mecca, decorated in the customary manner with symbols of the memorable journey: a ship, the holy city of Mecca, a lion, and a literary account of the event.

92. *The sites of many villages, especially those near the great centres of ancient Egyptian civilization, have been inhabited for thousands of years. Some villages were first built to house the artists and craftsmen who created the great monuments.*

93. Thebes West, the colourful houses of
generations of alabaster craftsmen,
self–styled archaeological guides and plain
tomb robbers.
The people of the villages of Thebes West
refused to move to smarter accommodation
provided by the government at New Qurna:
their houses may be humble, but their cellars
are pharaonic.

94. A colourful scarf with gold thread
enhances the brightness of her smile.
Educational opportunities have been
widened in recent years, but still a quarter of
Egyptian children never go to school.

95. Thebes West, an alabaster craftsman's
house, gaily painted with the symbols of his
trade and with the story of his pilgrimage to
Mecca. (pp. 150-151)

96. *A decorated camel at Giza. The guide is looking out for straying tourists on this confusing site, which has nine pyramids and many mastabas. The monuments are huge and visible, but the terrain between them is rough, so that a camel ride is your best bet.*

97. *A Bedouin camp in the Sinai Peninsula. The Bedouins' life style has changed little since they moved into Egypt in the wake of the Arab conquest in the seventh century.*

*98. Peasants in their traditional galabiyas
take shelter from the heat in a donkey stable
to discuss the order of the day.*

99. On the banks of the waterways, date palms and berseem, the grass used to feed livestock, are still the chief cultures, along with sugar cane and cotton. An old Turkish cemetery is left amid the crops.

100. The regular pattern of fields, irrigated by networks of canals edged by date palms, is unchanged since the time of the pharaohs.

101. An ill-assorted camel and ox are yoked together to draw the ancient wooden plough. The dark soil is rich in humus and the debris of thousands of years of habitation.

102. *Clean tap-water is now available throughout Egypt. Many people, however, still trust the water of the Nile and canals for a sip on a hot day or for brewing a pot of tea.*

103. Water lilies on the still canal surface. On the straight, well-trodden path, the peasant from the field, the shepherd from the pasture, head for home towards evening.

104. The most important fish on the Egyptian fish market is the Qarmoot (Clarius niloticus), which provides the main source of income for the traditional fishermen.

105. The fertile soil deposited by the Nile floods over the ages is now too scarce and precious to be wasted in brickmaking. Nowadays, sun-dried bricks are made from soils unsuitable for other uses, most commonly, sand.

106. Traditional life style among the peasants, the fellahin, will linger for many generations to come. The water buffalo, unknown to the ancients in the Mediterranean region, was introduced into Egypt by the Arabs. (pp. 160-161)

107. In the remotest areas and in the fertile Fayyum the wooden plough can still be seen in daily use. Lean draught oxen casily pull the scratch-plough, even on heavy clay soil, when guided by a skilled hand. (pp. 162-163)

108. *Mud-brick huts are gradually being replaced by the universal concrete-block house throughout the Mediterranean and the Third World. This Egyptian village on the bank of the Nile is a typical example of this development, which is changing the aspect of rural settlements.*

109. *Nile fishermen search the murky waters of the river near Cairo. Though heavily polluted, it still offers opportunities for a good catch. The Nile perch may reach over 6ft in length and 180lbs in weight.*

110. *Between the roads and canals, the square grid of fields with different crops, interspersed by rural settlements, creates the patchwork typical of the Nile Valley. Here, everything has been planned and worked out through thousands of years of toil.*

this time a more general level of nationalist sentiment had been aroused by a ghastly incident which took place at Denshawai, a small village in the Delta, in 1906. A party of British officers had gathered there for a day's sport pigeon-shooting. The local *fellahin* were outraged, believing that this was a deliberate attempt to deprive them of their staple diet, and they attacked the officers. One man died, and a *fellah* who had come to his aid as he lay wounded was beaten to death by British soldiers arriving on the scene, who thought he had murdered their fellow officer. All 'guilty' Egyptians were rounded up, tried, and given severe sentences which included hangings and floggings. These the villagers were compelled to watch.

Any affection the Egyptians may have had for Lord Cromer evaporated after this episode, and on his retirement, the following year, he left Egypt under armed protection. He was replaced by Eldon Gorst, a man experienced in Egyptian affairs, who considered that the post offered him a freedom of rulership which even India could not match. This speaks for itself in showing how little real influence the Egyptians had in their own affairs at this time.

The World Wars

Despite his high hopes, Gorst was an extremely unsuccessful governor, and lacked Cromer's political flair, but still the British grip on Egypt was too firm for the nationalists to loosen. His successor, Lord Kitchener, repressed nationalist forces while remaining a friend to the *fellahin* and their problems. When World War I broke out in 1914, domestic issues were put aside. The question of whether Egypt was a part of the British empire was raised, but left unanswered; a makeshift arrangement declared the country a British protectorate. Egypt officially remained neutral, but did in fact supply troops to defend the Suez Canal and to serve in Palestine and in France. Like other countries fighting in the war, it was not spared heavy loss of life.

After the war, Egypt's status was changed yet again: in 1922 it was declared an independent country bound to Britain by special treaty. By the Constitution of 1923, Egypt was to be a parliamentary democracy. The title of sultan, now held by Fuad, son of Khedive Ismail, was converted to that of king, but as a constitutional monarch he had limited powers, and British hold on the nation had not been relinquished, for Egypt was still a vital bridgehead for the empire. Further British interference in the country's affairs proved highly unwelcome, and the Anglo-Egyptian relationship lurched from crisis to crisis for several years.

As in 1914, however, the approach of a world war caused a shift in outlook. The British and the Egyptians had been locked into a kind of uneasy stalemate for years, but now it was imperative that relations should be improved. Under pressure from the nationalist movement led by Saad Zaghlul, founder of the Wafd party, Britain was prepared to compromise; the status of the high commissioner was reduced to that of ambassador and Egypt was given control over its own army, with the agreement that Britain should maintain a military presence in the Canal Zone to protect communications. With its new diplomatic freedom, Egypt chose to become a member of the League of Nations. Other agreements were also secured: the Suez Canal Company was to have at least two Egyptians on its board of directors, employ a minimum of 35 per cent of Egyptians in its labour force, and pay a concession of 300,000 Egyptian pounds per annum to the state.

During the inter-war period, fascism reared its ugly head in Egypt. Not one, but two parties of this type emerged: the Young Egypt party of

Ahmed Hussein, who were known as the Green Shirts and modelled on Mussolini's Black Shirts, and their rivals, the Blue Shirts, organized by the Wafd party. The two fought a series of pitched battles on university campuses, and soon after violence became rife between them, a third fascist movement of pro-royalist youth also appeared on the scene. Egyptian politics were now a terrifying muddle of intrigue and terrorism. The country was ruled by a new king, Farouk, who had come to the throne after the death of his father, Fuad, in 1936, and who himself showed fascist sympathies.

During the war Britain moved its forces back into Egypt, which became the basis of British military operations in the Middle East. Further outbreaks of pro-Nazi activity and fascism proved so dangerous that the King was ordered to suppress these activities. The demand provoked another governmental crisis, amidst deteriorating economic conditions and at a time of extreme danger to the Allied troops in the Western Desert. Egypt was already a target for air raid attacks, and the Germans were advancing ever closer, occupying Greece and Crete by 1940.

The following winter, shortages of food and clothing led to black marketeering and eventually food riots; by January 1942 there was not even enough bread to go round, despite rationing. The pro-Nazis had not been entirely subdued, and in 1942, as Rommel's forces approached, groups in Cairo could be heard shouting slogans in their favour. The British now forced Farouk to accept a Wafdist government, the best chance of maintaining internal security and order in the country.

As the Axis forces approached Alexandria, panic broke out. Those who were pro-British began to leave the country, while those who were anti-British stepped up their campaign. Caught between the two, Premier Nahas Pasha publicly declared his support for the Allies while at the same time privately preparing for a Nazi victory. As usual, there was no unanimity of purpose; the opposition party was plotting to discredit the Wafdists,

The opening of the Suez Canal, November 17, 1869.

and the King to maintain his own supremacy. Fortunately for Egypt, the threat of German invasion receded after the battle of el-Alamein in 1942, but the country remained a stronghold for Allied troops pushing back the Axis forces from the Middle East.

Egypt finally declared war on Germany in February 1945, but by this time the hostilities were almost over. Britain thus had no further need of a Wafd parliament to maintain stability, and so a coalition came to power. Just as this government was preparing the declaration of war, the Prime Minister was assassinated, so that it was his successor, Mahmud Fahmi el-Naqrashi, who was responsible for making the announcement public.

The war, and the British presence, had at least provided some sort of pressure to structure Egyptian political life, but when both these factors were removed, it rapidly fell into chaos. The old political groupings disintegrated, and into the vacuum tumbled all kinds of extremists, who were radical, religious, or fascist in outlook. Then attention turned to the Palestine question. Egypt had recently become a member of the United Nations, and, as a member of the Arab League, voted against the resolution to partition Palestine. In May 1948 Egyptian forces were sent to join other Arab troops in the area fighting against its implementation, where they engaged in acts of violence, including the blowing up of department stores and attacks against other British and Jewish targets.

Martial law was then enforced in Egypt until 1950, the year after the war in Palestine was lost and Egypt signed an armistice agreement supporting the new state of Israel. After its removal, political instability came to the fore once more, with a number of ephemeral governments forming and dissolving. Political factions in the country now included communists, Islamic fundamentalists, and anti-royalists; increasingly repressive measures were taken against agitators. In 1950 the Wafdist party was re-elected, and applied itself to improving conditions in rural and working class areas; its legislation and social measures covered sickness compensation, contracts of employment, cost of living allowances, and the redistribution of land to peasant farmers.

The Revolution

The shadow of trouble still hovered over the Suez Canal, and was later to develop into a full-blown crisis. Britain's Labour government had retained its control over the Canal Zone, despite the terms of the 1936 agreement, and the British military defended its presence there by strengthening the garrison against direct attacks and sabotage. By the end of 1951, sporadic anti-British demonstrations had developed into fully-fledged guerrilla warfare. In Cairo, both workers and students were in a state of violent agitation and threw all their grievances into demonstrations against the government, the King, and the British. At Ismailia, on 25 January, British troops surrounded the police headquarters at dawn, demanding the surrender of its occupants, who were among their prime suspects. They resisted, and the resulting attack left fifty Egyptians dead, and many more wounded.

The following day has since come to be known as Black Saturday. Cairo was put to the torch by a rampaging mob who set about destroying all the British and foreign-owned property they could find. If the government did incite these riots, as has sometimes been suggested, they surely lived to regret it in the havoc and destruction that followed. Rather than risk the appearance of British troops to quell the populace, the government imposed martial law.

The King's hope for restoring order during the dark period that followed lay in the army. After the Palestinian troubles, he had given refuge to a number of ex-Nazi army officers whom he now used to try and strengthen the upper echelons of the army. With the main body of soldiers, he had little or no contact, and failed to make any new impression on them by raising their pay. The army, as it happened, was already hatching its own underground political organization. This was the association of the Free Officers, its nucleus a small group of young men who had formed a close alliance while at military college and during active service. Among the founding members there was a Lieutenant Colonel Nasser, and a Lieutenant Colonel Sadat.

Nasser was the first chairman of the party formed in 1949, and held the post till 1952. The first small group was growing rapidly, its members bitter over the incompetence of Egypt's rulers, and ambitious to do better. Farouk had already lost much of his popularity, changing from a handsome, youthful figure into a debauched middle-aged monarch, who spent extravagantly at Mediterranean resorts while the vast majority of his subjects languished in poverty. Sensing the threat from the Free Officers, Farouk endeavoured to curb the movement, but he failed; a coup was staged at midnight on 22 July 1952, and on the following day Colonel Sadat announced the success of the revolution over the radio. King Farouk was forced to abdicate, and to flee into exile with his wife and son.

The New Republic

In 1953, the monarchy was abolished and Egypt was proclaimed a republic. The Free Officers had transformed themselves into the Revolutionary Command Council, with General Naguib as its leader and Gamal Abdel Nasser as prime minister. But the birth of a new nation was not easy. 'The world's oldest monarchy became, for the time being, the world's youngest republic,' as President Naguib put it.

And who were this new nation, the Egyptians? Plainly the ancient stock that had peopled Egypt in the days of the pharaohs had altered beyond recognition. Many nationalities — Turks, Arabs, Kurds, Caucasians, Europeans and black Africans — had poured into Egypt. The ancient Coptic language had been superseded by Greek, Arabic and Turkish, and the gods of old supplanted first by Christianity and then by Islam.

The religion of the Prophet had taken root, however, and one thing was certain: the new republic would be based upon Islamic principles, and thus maintain its alliance with the Arab world. But the culture absorbed from Europe would also continue to form a part of Egyptian life and outlook, even though the urge to ape European values began to diminish as Egypt established its independent identity. As Nasser was to remark: 'Building factories is easy, building hospitals and schools is possible, but building a nation of men is a hard and difficult task.'

The first years of the republic were indeed hard. Opposition from outside the party came from the Muslim Brethren, a fundamentalist religious group whose members were to be found in all sections of society, and quarrels from within clouded the comradeship that had led the Council to victory. Naguib was its first president, and Nasser his deputy, but although Naguib was a popular figure, it was Nasser who triumphed in the dispute between them, assuming the presidency in 1954.

Following an assassination attempt upon Nasser's life in October 1954, over a thousand alleged conspirators of the Muslim Brethren were tried by military courts. A wave of arrests left prisons bursting at the seams, with some three thousand political prisoners held by 1955. Even

Naguib did not escape suspicion; Nasser accused him of being on over-friendly terms with the Brethren, and had him placed under house arrest. Jewish doctors and lawyers were also taken by force, some to be executed, and others to be sent to labour camps.

By 1956 a more settled era was dawning. The country was given a new constitution, and universal male suffrage was granted. A National Assembly was formed, drawing its members from each area of the country. President Nasser became a prominent figure in world affairs as one of the founders of the policy of non-alignment. He was a natural leader, popular and trusted, and no one loved Egypt better than he did. A broad education had created in him the certainty that Egypt's true strength was still only latent, and was now ready to be tapped after hundreds of years of foreign servitude. The best means to achieve this, he believed, was 'Arab socialism', which meant state intervention in all domains.

Nasser certainly had to prove himself a statesman capable of handling international affairs, since both the Suez Crisis and war with Israel erupted during his period in office. The Suez had remained an issue ever since it was first opened nearly a hundred years before, and was still partially controlled by outside forces. In 1956, angered by the withdrawal of promises by Britain, the United States and the World Bank to fund the building of the Aswan High Dam, Nasser seized the assets of the Suez Canal Company and nationalized it.

The prospect of throwing off the final remnants of imperial domination in Egypt caused great excitement. But Britain and France, in collusion with Israel, decided to use force to reclaim the Canal, despite warnings from both the United States and the Soviet Union. This was a serious miscalculation, condemned by the world at large and afterwards regretted. The

Edward Lane: Bridal procession.

Egyptians lost almost their entire air force and the allies were advancing through the Canal Zone before a United Nations emergency resolution persuaded them to halt their progress, and leave the Canal in Egyptian hands. Egypt now moved further towards agreements with other Arab nations, signing a joint defence agreement with Syria and becoming increasingly anti-Western in its outlook. Nasser also began to befriend the communist bloc; let down by the western powers over the building of the dam, he turned for assistance to the Soviet Union, which was happy to oblige. President Khrushchev himself came to celebrate the first stage of its completion, and the Russians continued to aid Egypt under the Nasser regime.

The Six-Day War with Israel, though, was a disaster for Nasser's government. In 1967 Egypt banded with Syria and Jordan to attack Israel, since the Palestine question was still unresolved in their opinion. Egypt and Israel had already engaged in undercover hostilities, but not until now did Egypt feel ready to take on full-scale war. Events proved that it was in fact far from ready; Israel defeated the aggressors in less than a week, and in that short space of time each of the three nations lost territory: Egypt the entire Sinai Peninsula, with its valuable oil wells, Syria the Golan Heights, and Jordan nearly all its arable land.

The nation's faith in Nasser was profoundly shaken, and only by branding a number of army generals as scapegoats did he survive to control the country for another three years. His death came early, in 1970, at the age of fifty-two, the stress of the Israeli conflict having affected his health, which, as a diabetic, was already poor. During these last few years the strength of his regime declined, and there were further hostilities with Israel, resulting in casualties and heavy bombing of Egypt.

The Sadat Era

Nasser was succeeded in office by his old military friend and colleague, Anwar el-Sadat. Sadat began by clearing himself a space for action, dismissing influential ministers and throwing out the Soviets, who departed from Egypt leaving unfinished projects and half-constructed buildings in their wake. He sought the friendship of the richer, more conservative Arab nations, and concentrated on attracting more foreign capital into the country. At home he attempted to remove the repression that had built up during the Nasser period, calling his policy the Corrective Movement.

He was still left with the old Palestinian problem to wrestle with. An earlier agreement with Israel did not hold, and in 1973 he ordered the Egyptian army to attack the Israeli troops. The battle took place on 6 October, the Jewish feast of Yom Kippur, the name by which this brief war is now known. The military successes of the first few days did much to restore the pride of the Egyptian people. In fact, both sides suffered heavy loss of life. The Yom Kippur War prompted fresh negotiations between Israel and Egypt, which began with the mediation of the American envoy, Dr Henry Kissinger, and ended with the signing of the Camp David peace agreement in 1979 under the auspices of US President Jimmy Carter. Before that, in 1977, Sadat had bravely made an unprecedented visit to Jerusalem, where he addressed the Knesset and struck a chord in the hearts of millions around the world, if not of the Israelis, by his talk of human equality in the sight of God.

Such an advance towards peace was not enthusiastically received by the fanatical anti-Jewish element in Egypt, and Sadat met fierce opposition from these and other extreme political movements. He was, in a sense, the victim of his popularity. As his vanity increased, so he became less tolerant, clamping down mercilessly on both Islamic fundamentalists and communists. The intransigence of Israel, which forced Sadat to make many concessions, increased his isolation in the Arab world. In 1981 he was assassinated by Islamic extremists during a military parade in Cairo.

Into the Future

His deputy, and former close associate, Hosni Mubarak was elected as the new president in October of that year. Perhaps Egypt was tired for the time being of charismatic leaders such as Nasser and Sadat, for Mubarak arrived with a reputation as honest, worthy, and uninspired. He freed all political prisoners, and set about restoring peace domestically, and good relations with the Soviet Union and other Arab nations, while still remaining on friendly terms with the West. As of 1987, Mubarak was elected for a further six-year term as president, a post which is still no easy ride. Although he has taken steps to integrate Muslim fundamentalists into the government, in October 1990 the President of the Egyptian Parliament was assassinated, and recent successes of religious extremists in the Muslim world may be an omen of troubled times to come.

Edward Lane: Women and children of the lower classes.

Traditional Culture

Like nearly every country in the world, Egypt is influenced by western ways, but the ancient pattern of culture, which endured for centuries, can still be found in many aspects of everyday life. To see this more clearly, it is helpful to examine accounts of Egyptian life written at an earlier date, when the traditional picture was still more or less intact. The best of these are found in the writings of visitors who came to Egypt before the end of the nineteenth century, for it is often foreigners to a country who take the trouble to observe and note down details which are commonplace to those living there. Before looking at the most up-to-date developments in Egypt, which are described in the next chapter, we will therefore try to distinguish the flavour of traditional Egyptian life, whose leisurely pace still underlies the frenetic, superimposed rhythms of modern city bustle.

One of the prime sources available is Edward Lane's magnificent work *The Manners and Customs of the Modern Egyptians*, published in London in 1836. Most visitors to Egypt at the time were chiefly interested in its ancient monuments, but Lane was deeply fascinated by Egypt as a living country, and meticulously recorded what he found. Another excellent publication, *Egypt - A Traveller's Anthology*, edited by Christopher Pick (John Murray 1991), contains a fascinating collection of eye-witness accounts of life in Egypt, many from the pre-republican era. Both books have proved immensely valuable in providing illustrations of traditional Egyptian culture for this chapter.

It is worth saying a little more about Edward Lane, since his contribution to the study of Egypt is unique. Lane came to Egypt for three years in 1825, and for another two years in 1833 to compile one of the most complete accounts of Egyptian culture ever made. Although Egypt had been subject to both French and British influence since the Napoleonic invasion in 1798, life outside the major cities was little affected and Lane saw Egypt as it was at the end of a long period of Ottoman rule. He was a self-taught oriental scholar, fluent in Arabic, with professional artistic skills which he was able to put to good use in painting the scenes that he encountered. Intended for the Church by his parents, he escaped genteel English society for something very different; in Egypt he adopted native dress and, as he looked somewhat Mediterranean in appearance, he was able to get close to the Egyptian people in a way that few outsiders could. 'Lane's Egyptian life was merely the preparation for the great work he had set before himself, namely to make Egyptians known to the world as they never had been before,' stated Alexander Gardner in his introduction to the 1895 edition of Lane's book, which covers, among other topics, Egypt's geography, population, education, culture, law, religion, domestic life, entertainment and trade.

The People and Language

Egypt was, of course, firmly established as an Arabic country in Lane's time. He pointed out however that it made a unique contribution to Arab culture, and that Cairo should be regarded as the leading Arab city of the day:

'The manners and customs of its inhabitants are particularly interesting, as they are a combination of those which prevail most generally in the towns of Arabia, Syria and the whole of Northern Africa, and in great degree in Turkey. There is no other place in which we can obtain so complete a knowledge of the most civilized class of the Arabs.'

Although Egyptians are classed as Arabs, their blood is mixed and a considerable physical difference is found between the Egyptians and the

113. Abu Simbel, the temple of Ramesses II. Since its rescue by a UNESCO team of international experts in 1968, it has been one of Egypt's major tourist attractions.

114. Aerial view of the new site of the Abu Simbel temples. The artificial hills of reinforced concrete create the illusion of the natural rocks into which the two temples were originally hewn. Abu Simbel is today a thriving township, a kind of Egyptian Las Vegas, enjoying the revenues from thousands of visitors who come flocking by air and road across 250 mi. of desert. (pp. 178-179)

115. The Great Temple of Ramesses II at Abu Simbel in Nubia, a region of great economic importance in the time of the New Kingdom. After the passing of ancient Egyptian civilization, the site was forgotten until rediscovered by the Swiss orientalist Johann Burckhardt in 1813. The raising of the Abu Simbel temples to prevent their inundation was carried out in 1968 by a team of German, Italian, French and Swedish engineers at a cost of 40 million dollars. (pp. 180-181)

116. Abu Simbel, temple of Ramesses II. Seated figures of the Pharaoh tower above visitors as they enter the dark interior of the rock temple. Amelia B. Edwards, a noted British Nile traveller in the late nineteenth century, wrote: 'Ramesses the Great, if he was as much like his portraits as his portraits are like each other, must have been one of the handsomest men, not only of his own day, but of all history...'

117. Abu Simbel, temple of Ramesses II. In her famous book 'A Thousand Miles up the Nile', published in 1877, Amelia Edwards wrote of this temple: 'Nothing in Egyptian sculpture is perhaps quite as wonderful as the way in which these Abu Simbel artists dealt with the thousands of tons of material to which they here gave human form. Consummate masters of effect, they knew precisely what to do, and what to leave undone.'

118. Luxor. On the right-hand side of the plinth of the colossal statue of Ramesses II, still intact, is this relief representing the union of Upper and Lower Egypt. The papyrus of Upper Egypt and the lotus of Lower Egypt are being tied together by figures representing the two countries.

119. A relief in the Geat Temple of Abu Simbel symbolizing Lower Egypt in the act of union with Upper Egypt.

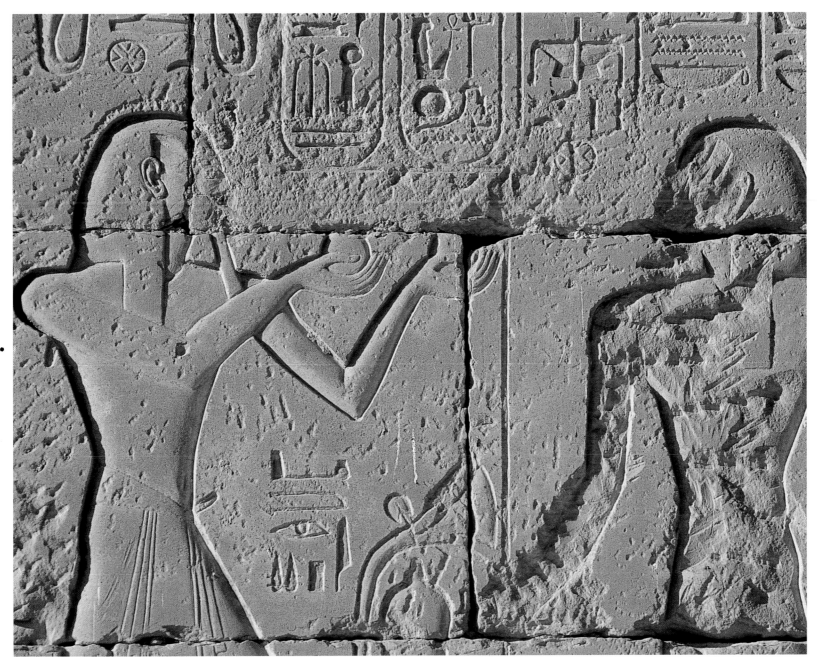

120. Thebes West, Medinet Habu, a relief of
Ramesses III making an offering to a deity
which has been defaced by religious fanatics.
The mortuary temple of the great
warrior-king is covered with reliefs
celebrating his triumphs. The Pharaoh's
actual tomb is in the Valley of the Kings.

121. Egyptian hieroglyphics are now
comparatively easy to read. They were first
deciphered by the Frenchman Jean François
Champollion (1790-1832),who also carried
out the first scientific survey of Egyptian
monuments. The results of his work were
published by his brother, Jacques,after his
early death.

122. Abu Simbel, the façade of the temple of Hathor and Nefertari, known as the Small Temple, hewn out of the cliff face. Like the Great Temple of Abu Simbel, it was moved uphill when Lake Nasser was created and half of Nubia vanished forever under its waters.

123. Abu Simbel, temple of Queen Nefertari. In a statue to the left of the entrance, Ramesses II wears the crown of Upper Egypt.

124. Abu Simbel, temple of Queen Nefertari. This portrait of Ramesses II on the right of the entrance shows him wearing the double crown of Upper and Lower Egypt.

125. Abu Simbel, the temple of Nefertari. Her husband, Pharaoh Ramesses II, seems to be stepping out of his niche beside the entrance. Six colossal statues, about 38 ft high, are set in the niches of the façade. Each group comprises Nefertari flanked by Ramesses.

126. Deep inside the Great Temple of Abu Simbel is the sanctuary with four seated divinities facing the rising sun. The figures from left to right represent Ptah, Amon-Ra, the deified Ramesses II, and Re-Harakhte. Twice a year, in February and October, the first rays of the sun strike the face of Ramesses II. (pp. 188-189)

127. Abu Simbel, the Small Temple of Queen Nefertari, 130 yds from the Great Temple of her husband, Ramesses II. The structure is nearly 100 ft wide and 40 ft high. At the feet of the royal couple stand much smaller images of their children. (pp. 190-191)

people of Arabia. Lane noted that even within Egypt, physical appearance varied according to the region:

'In Cairo and throughout the northern provinces, those who have not been exposed to the sun have a yellowish but very clear complexion and soft skin; the rest are of a considerably darker and coarser complexion. The people of Middle Egypt are of a more tawny colour, and those of the more southern provinces are of a deep bronze or brown complexion — darkest towards Nubia, where the climate is hottest.'

But nowhere, Lane remarked, did he find fat Egyptians, except for a few indolent city-dwellers. Differences in skin colour are still obvious in Egypt today, and although the subject of colour and caste is a delicate matter to discuss, nevertheless the fact remains that it is rare to find a really dark-skinned person among the wealthier classes, or holding a top post in a Cairo hotel or club. Compared with other North African nations, however, Egyptians are darker in appearance, for Egypt has always had a strong connection with the main African continent. This is partly due to its geography, the Nile acting like a great avenue which has been travelled by people from different ethnic regions.

The language of Lane's time was, as it is today, Arabic, and Lane ranks it inferior in purity of grammar and pronunciation to that spoken by the Bedouins of Arabia, but better by far than the Arabic of Syria and incomparably superior to that of the western Arabs! Most of the differences between regional Arabic are of interest only to the linguist, but one that is easily noticed is the pronunciation of the 'g' (as we should write it), the fifth letter of the alphabet, which is hard in Egypt and soft in most other Arabic-speaking nations. Egyptian pronunciation is, in fact, the more ancient of the two.

Traditional Dress

The costumes described by Lane can still be found today, even though growing numbers of the population now wear western-style clothes. Traditionally, there were differences of detail between even apparently similar costumes, giving clues as to the wealth, status and religious persuasion of the wearer. Some of these details were like fine points of grammar which only the native speaker can appreciate. The way a woman would hold her cloak, the fit of her dress, and the amount of ankle exposed, would speak as eloquently as any language to those who could understand it. For us today, it is probably enough to recognize some of the basic styles of Egyptian dress, and to realize that subtle differences between them may have meanings that we cannot altogether fathom. Certain of these old distinctions of dress have been eroded, and others have grown up in their place.

The Prophet forbade the wearing of trousers, and thus traditional dress for men consists of a full-length shirt, known as *galabiya*. This is the most popular item of dress today; often made of striped or plain cotton, it gives the typical Egyptian rural scene a strongly biblical aspect to western eyes. In the past the costume was completed by a striped, sleeveless tunic, worn loose and open over the *galabiy*a, and known as a *sudeyree*. Over this again, a *kaftan* was sometimes worn, with full-length sleeves, and round his waist a man would wrap a coloured shawl. Though decorative, this would also have a more practical purpose, acting as a belt to hold a knife or a gun. This was the full male costume, but that of the *fellah* was usually simpler, consisting of a pair of loose drawers reaching to just below the knee, covered by an ample full-length shirt with wide sleeves, made of blue linen, cotton or wool, known as a *zaaboot*.

128. Abu Simbel, the third of four 60ft-high seated figures of Ramesses II on the façade of his temple. The Pharaoh faces the rising sun with an inscrutable expression, careless of the graffiti tattooed on his body by generations of visitors.

Headwear for men was traditionally of great importance, and although its significance is now diminished, examples of the different types can still be seen. A small cotton cap was worn underneath the *fez*, the classical red cylindrical felt hat, more correctly known as a *tarboosh*. The *tarboosh* would be wrapped around with a cloth which indicated the status of the wearer, green signifying that its owner was a descendant of the Prophet. Men of religious orders wore an especially wide turban, called the *mukla*.

Today the main type of costume worn is the *galabiya*, its type varying somewhat depending upon the wealth of the wearer. The most common has a long neckline, and a V-shaped slit which may be left open or fastened with buttons. It has wide sleeves, and broadens out to a hem just above the ankles. The width of the hem at the ankle and the wrist varies, and is generally wider among country dwellers than urban folk. Likewise, the shape of the V-neck can indicate whether the wearer is of a traditional or more modern outlook; those who consider themselves sophisticated sport a neckline more similar to a European shirt. From the latter, two distinct new styles of *galabiya* have thus emerged; the *galabiya frangi*, and the *galabiya sandarini*, developed largely by workers and students returning home from abroad.

Women's dress was observed in fine detail by Lane, who noted also that women liked to blacken their eyelids with kohl and stain their hands and feet with red henna, practices common in other Arabic countries such as Morocco. Egyptian henna powder, derived from the leaves of a tree growing along the banks of the Nile, was much in demand abroad. The practice of Islam demands that women cover themselves almost entirely in public, and thus they will naturally tend to accentuate the only parts of the body left exposed — the eyes, the hands and the feet.

The basic dress worn today is usually home-made and cut from linen

Edward Lane: The procession to the bath – a pre-nuptial custom.

194

or cotton cloth, with a heavier kind of cotton called *kustor*, which is subsidized by the government, being used for winter wear. Two main variations are prevalent today. The first is the *galabiya bi wist*, found chiefly in the region of the Nile stretching from Beni Suef to Asyut, and consisting of a long, waisted dress; the second hails from the Delta and the Cairo area, and is an equally long dress, but this time with a yoked bodice, and known as the *galabiya bi suffra*.

Many of the types of female dress described by Lane have not survived although regional differences are still encountered: a kind of outfit described by Lane as 'walking or riding attire', otherwise known as *tezyeereh*, can occasionally be seen in Cairo and elsewhere. This is composed of a very wide black silk robe called the *habarah*, which covers everything apart from a small area of the face, and a *burko*, or full-length veil of white muslin, concealing all but the eyes. In the years following the establishment of the republic, it became far less common for women to wear any sort of a veil, but with the growth of fundamentalism, the custom is becoming more widespread even among college students.

Whatever their dress, all women today wear some form of head covering from an early age. The simplest is a scarf, the *sharb*, which is a square folded into a triangle, made of plain material, black or brightly-coloured. It covers the hair, the ends being taken around the back of the head, brought forward and tied in a knot on the forehead. In the north it is customary to wear a second scarf, a *tarha*, on top of this; a *tarha* is a black rectangle of cloth, some two to four yards in length, which is wrapped around the head and the ends left to hang down the back. For formal occasions, a woman may wear a *shaal*, or *shawl*, of heavier material wrapped around the head and flowing over her shoulders.

Edward Lane: Ladies riding.

Relationships and the Family

'The women of Egypt have the character of being the most licentious in their feelings of all females who lay any claim to be considered as members of a civilized nation...' writes a shocked Edward Lane, and carries on to splutter indignantly that 'the generality of husbands in Egypt endeavour to increase the libidinous feelings of their wives by every means in their power.' The excess of Egyptian passion, he concludes, may be blamed both on a hot climate and on the practice of polygamy!

Times have changed, and it may be that the ardent sexual desires of Egyptian women were shocking only to the nineteenth-century Englishman who believed that true ladies felt no such thing. Customs have changed, too, and polygamy is now practically non-existent in modern Egypt although a Muslim may, in theory, take up to four wives, provided that he can keep them all and treat them equally. Lane found that polygamy was common among the lower classes, probably for economic reasons: the peasant classes worked for a living, and thus a man with four wives had four extra pairs of hands to till the soil, whereas a rich man was expected to support his wife and any additional spouse was thus a drain on his resources.

Where the Islamic code is strictly practised, unlicensed sexual relations are severely frowned upon and adultery on the part of the wife brings down the full weight of the law. 'Adultery is the most severely visited,' says Lane, 'but to establish a charge of this crime against a wife, four eye-witnesses are necessary.' Perhaps this gave leeway for discreet extramarital activity, but one fears for the woman who was maliciously or falsely accused because, in Lane's day, the adulteress was condemned to be put to death by stoning.

Modesty in public is one of the chief demands made of Muslim women, and traditionally a woman might not unveil except in front of her husband or close relatives. However, in reading both Gustave Flaubert and Edward Lane, we may find a rather different picture painted of life in Cairo, where even outward appearances of discretion were often discarded. Lane remarks: 'I believe that in Egypt the women are generally under less restraint than in any other country of the Turkish empire; so that it is not uncommon to see females of the lower orders flirting and jesting with men in public, and men laying their hands upon them very freely.'

Until the 1952 revolution, women of a wealthy household lived in a harem. They kept to their own quarters and no males except the husband, children and certain other relations were allowed to enter. Apart from the wives, there would also be servants and slaves present, perhaps the master's concubines, and even, in some establishments, a eunuch to keep an eye upon the ladies. Nineteenth-century travellers also noticed with wonder that both railway trains and opera houses provided for female seclusion: a closed room within the railway carriage and gauze veils stretched across the theatre boxes so that their occupants might see, but not be seen. Our usual picture of a harem as a place of exotic luxury, full of sumptuous silks and brocade sofas for lounging on, may be something of a myth; Mabel Caillard, recalling her life in Egypt, remarks drily that on the many occasions that she paid social visits to harems she found that they had 'heavy and comfortless formality', their occupants sitting stiffly on hard, high couches covered with dreary material.

Marriage, and family life, however, is still as popular in Egypt as it was when Lane wrote that 'to abstain from marrying when a man has attained a sufficient age, and when there is no just impediment, is esteemed by the Egyptians improper and even disreputable'. In his day it was common for girls to be married off young, at about twelve or thirteen; these were arranged marriages, with a dowry as an essential element of the contract. Today, the marriage age is much later, and partners are freely chosen, among the professional classes at least, but the marriage procedure still falls into two parts: the drawing up of the contract, later followed by the religious ceremony itself.

Marriages were traditionally performed with much elaborate festivity, involving a public procession of the bride and her female relatives decked out in their best finery; the bride might be led under a canopy of gold-embroidered cloth to her nuptials. However, sometimes only a few words were said to legitimize the relationship. This was often a way of setting up a short-term affair without invoking official disapproval. Divorce, too, has always been easy under Islamic law — for the man at least — so that marriage became a succession of sexual adventures for some. Lane commented:

'That the facility of divorce has depraving effects upon both sexes may be easily imagined. There are many men in this country who in the course of ten years have married as many as twenty or more wives; and women not far advanced in age who have been wives to a dozen or more men successively. I have heard of men who have been in the habit of marrying a new wife almost every month. A person may do this although possessed of very little property. He may choose, from among the females of the lower orders in the streets of Cairo, a handsome young widow or divorced woman who will consent to become his wife for a dowry of about ten shillings.'

Children have always been much loved, but in earlier times extreme poverty sometimes resulted in their being sold, presumably as slaves. Lane tells us: 'A young family is sometimes an insupportable burden to poor parents. Hence it is not a very rare occurrence in Egypt for children to be publicly carried about for sale, by their mothers or by women employed by the fathers.' Today's children may be poor, but they are unlikely to be thus wrenched away from their families. They may run naked up till about six or seven years of age, after which time they are dressed as miniature adults. Considering how much love and care Egyptians lavish on their offspring, the visitor may find it odd to see children dirty and dressed in rags, playing in the dust or scampering around a rubbish heap, but in fact to avert the 'evil eye' the child may deliberately be kept scruffy. It is thought that if he or she is too beautiful, it may attract admiration and envy which can cause the child, however innocent, to fall ill and even die.

Circumcision, usually performed at the age of five or six, is the great rite of passage for boys. The ceremony involves much dressing up and congratulation, and the parents usually parade the boy around the streets to receive the good wishes of the local people. But while the religious practice of male circumcision remains acceptable today, that of female circumcision, a common tradition in central Africa and among the peasants of Egypt, has aroused a storm of opposition. Unlike the simple operation involved for boys, circumcision for girls is a procedure of severe mutilation, often resulting in lifelong pain and gynaecological problems. Unfortunately fighting to retain the tradition are the older women themselves, who fear that their daughters will be thought ugly if left uncircumcised. Certain Islamic scholars have banded against the practice, pointing out that nowhere is it sanctioned by Islam, nor did it originate within Islam.

Sons are named by their fathers, daughters by their mothers. Traditional names are those of the Prophet, his family, and followers, such as

Mohammed, Ahmed, Mustafa, Ali, Hassan, Hoseyn, Ibrahim, Ismail, Ishak, Yakob, Moosa, Daood and Suleyman for boys, and Khadige, Aisha, Amne, Fatme, or Zeyneb for girls. Girls can also be named after a flower or precious object, or their names can be epithets such as Mahboobe (Beloved), Mebrooken (Blessed), or Nefeese (Precious).

Daily Life

The traditional work of the *fellah* on the land has been briefly described in Chapter I. Here, Lane paints a picture of women's work:
'Their chief occupations are the preparing of the husband's food, fetching water, spinning cotton, linen, or woollen yarn, and making the fuel called *gelleh*, which is composed of the dung of cattle, kneaded with chopped straw, and formed into round flat cakes: these they stick upon the walls or roofs of their houses or upon the ground, to dry in the sun, and then use for heating their ovens and for other purposes.'
Women may make a little extra money by taking their produce, some surplus eggs, or home-made cakes and cheeses, to market. Market day is a great social occasion, with goods being sold not only from stalls but by itinerant peddlers, all cheerfully shouting out the merits of their wares. In the cities, permanent bazaars are the focus of daily transactions, the place to buy fruit, meat, vegetables, spices, cloth, pots, jewelry and metalwork. Some bazaars and shopping areas retain the medieval tradition of each trade occupying one area; the coppersmiths of Cairo, for instance, may be found all ranged along one street.
A traditional feature of urban living was the communal bath, another focus of social life and something to be enjoyed in a leisurely manner. Sophia Poole, sister of Edward Lane, was dismayed to find that women of all ages wandered around together with not a stitch of clothing on. She soon learnt to rush through such distressing scenes of public nudity to one of the private chambers on hire! First came the steam bath, during which an attendant gently kneaded the bather, and would crack her joints on request (a version of modern osteopathy). Then she might choose to be rubbed, the attendant's hands now being encased in a woollen bag, after which she could be lathered with a mixture of soap and palm-tree fibers, known as *leef*. The Egyptian bath, concluded Sophia Poole, was a most salubrious and satisfactory experience, provided that the Englishwoman could escape both from the nakedness that would offend her propriety, and from the shouting of children that would offend her ears.

Food and Drink

In an old-fashioned, upper-class household, the husband would not eat with his wife and children. Even among the *fellahin*, there were many, Lane tells us, who never took a meal with their families. The fondness among Egyptian men for tobacco was already very marked in his day, for he says, 'the pipe and the cup of coffee are enjoyed by almost all persons who can afford such luxuries very early in the morning, and often during the day. There are many men who are scarcely ever seen without a pipe either in their hand or carried behind them by a servant.' Today, almost every Egyptian male smokes, and a *shibuk*, or pipe, can be hired in the local coffee shop.

Often coffee was all that was taken for breakfast, but for those preferring an early meal, Lane describes a breakfast of bread, eggs, butter, cheese, and clotted cream, or of a *fateereh*, a rich buttery pastry made of very thin leaves of dough folded over and over, with perhaps some honey or sugar poured over it. This would be the breakfast of a well-off family. From Lane, we can also find out something about the typical food of the peasant classes:

'Their food chiefly consists of bread (made of millet or of maize), milk, new cheese, eggs, small salted fish, cucumbers and melons and gourds of a great variety of kinds, onions and leeks, beans, chick-peas, lupins, the fruit of the black egg-plant, lentils etc., dates (both fresh and dried) and pickles. Most of the vegetables they eat in a crude state. When the maize (or Indian corn) is nearly ripe, many ears of it are plucked, toasted or baked, and eaten thus by the peasants. Rice is too dear to be an article of common food for the fallaheen (*fellahin*), and flesh-meat they seldom taste... It is surprising to observe how simple and poor is the diet of the Egyptian peasantry, and yet how robust and healthy most of them are, and how severe is the labour which they can undergo.'

The Islamic religion strictly forbids the eating of pork; as in Judaism, the pig is considered to be a filthy animal. Other meat killed for human consumption must be ritually slaughtered, its throat cut, and the cry of 'God is most great!' sent up by the person carrying out the deed. Alcoholic drinks are prohibited, intoxication also being a sign of falling away from the true religion, but not all Islamic countries have kept strictly to this code. Egypt

Edward Lane: A party at dinner or supper.

was fairly liberal in this respect even during the more orthodox days of the nineteenth century:

'There are a few who transgress in this flagrant manner. *Booweh* or *boozah*, which is an intoxicating liquor made with barley-bread, crumbled, mixed with water, strained, and left to ferment, is commonly drunk by the boatmen of the Nile and by other persons of the lower orders.' This leaves little doubt as to where the popular English word for drink — booze — comes from! Today, Egyptian beer, 'Stella', is very popular, and it is not unknown for Muslims to claim they are keeping the word of the Prophet by never touching wine: they drink whisky instead!

In Lane's day, Nile water was all that was on offer at most meal tables. 'The water of the Nile is remarkably good, but that of all the wells in Cairo and in other parts of Egypt is slightly brackish.' Although Lane may have enjoyed supping river water, the health risks involved were severe, as will be discussed in the next chapter. Nowadays, water is piped into the villages so that safe drinking water is on hand throughout the country.

Class and Rank

That there were sharp differences between the social customs of the different classes will have already become obvious. Ways of describing status were more important in the time of Mehmet Ali, the period during which Lane visited Egypt, so that any male of even modest rank, on attaining to manhood, was given the honorary title of *sheikh* meaning 'elder', or 'aged person'. The word *sheikh* was also used more specifically to describe a man of religion or learning.

Descendants of the Prophet, who were to be found in all walks of life, were called *shereef*, and anyone who had made the prescribed pilgrimage to Mecca, was known as *hagg*, which is still the case today. For women, a common form of address was *sitt*, meaning lady or mistress of the household.

The poorer the family, the greater the degree of female subjugation. Lane observed that when such a husband and wife went out, 'she generally walks behind him: and if there be anything for either of them to carry, it is usually borne by the wife, unless it be merely a pipe or stick'. Such a practice was not unique to Egypt, but was also common in other Mediterranean countries.

Real slavery is, officially at least, outlawed in the Egypt of today, but it was a long-standing feature of Egyptian history, as we have already seen. It was common during Mehmet Ali's reign, when there was a flourishing slave trade stemming from Abyssinia and black Africa. Abuse of young girls and children was frequent: 'Most... are abominably corrupted by the Gellabs, or slave-traders, of Upper Egypt and Nubia, by whom they are brought from their native countries. There are very few of the age of eight or nine years who have not suffered brutal violence; and so severely did these children, particularly the Abyssinians, and boys as well as girls, feel the treatment which they endure from the Gellabs, that many instances occur of their drowning themselves during the voyage down the Nile.'

These were Lane's observations. Another visitor to Egypt at about the same period, William Müller, visited a Cairo slave market, where he found thirty or forty children and youngsters for sale in an open courtyard. Upstairs, in the adjoining house, the most beautiful of the females were kept; if a buyer showed interest in one of these she would be stripped naked for his appraisal. Once in an Egyptian family, however, the lot of a slave often improved, and here she would be considered a permanent part of the

134. *Cairo Citadel, the French Clock, a gift in 1845 to Ali Pasha from Emperor Louis Philippe of France, who clearly made an effort to suit the recipient's taste.*

135. *Cairo, Islamic statements against the backdrop of the mosque of Sultan Hassan, a masterpiece of Arab architecture. Raised by this Mamluk ruler in the mid-fourteenth century, it is also the seat of the four orthodox schools of jurisprudence of Sunnite Islam.*

136. Cairo is a city of contrasts, where ancient mosques with their slender minarets rise serenely above the roar of traffic, where modern high-rise buildings overlook tumbledown dwellings. It is the largest city on the African continent, and still growing fast.

137. A busy city junction. In the absence of traffic lights and zebra crossings, there is a constant noisy stream of vehicles, which pedestrians must dodge through as best they can, often climbing over them to get across the street.

138. Wherever in the eastern Mediterranean Mehmet (Mohammed) Ali Pasha held sway, men still play backgammon in public places. Men-only games and entertainments predominate throughout the Mediterranean lands.

139. One of thousands of shops in Egyptian bazaars selling pseudo-Turkish paraphernalia intended for tourists.

140. A brassware shop in Khan el-Khalili, the largest of Cairo's bazaars, founded in about 1400. Shops are arranged in narrow streets according to crafts. Often the goods are made on the spot.

141. A market street in Cairo with a colourful banner of the type used to decorate the streets for festivals and funerals.

142. As one climbs up to the Cairo Citadel, the minarets of the Sultan Hassan and el-Rifai mosques seem to rise from behind the balustrade. From the top there is a splendid view of the city, reaching as far as the Great Pyramids. (pp. 216–217)

143. A truck on the way to the camel market. A good camel may cost as much as 3,000 Egyptian pounds or more. Though largely replaced by all manner of vehicles, the animal is still invaluable for carrying sugar cane and cotton crops across rough terrain.

144. *A baker's boy carrying loaves of bread is a common sight in the streets of Cairo. Egyptian food draws on Arab and Turkish traditions. The peasants' diet is simple but healthy, whereas city folk tend to overindulge in sweetmeats.*

145. Some are lucky enough to afford a game of golf within sight of the Great Pyramids.

*146. A smart sports club at Giza. It must take
considerable effort and expense to keep the
turf green here on the Giza plateau.*

147. The Egyptian Museum of Cairo is set in its own grounds, a garden full of statues, including one of Auguste Mariette, founder of the collection. Whereas the Greeks and Romans admired and collected Egyptian antiquities, not so the Arabs and Turks, who used the stones from ancient monuments to build their own palaces, as the Popes did in Rome.

148. The Egyptian Museum of Cairo, a view of the ground-floor atrium from the first-floor gallery. When the French scholar Auguste Mariette was made Director of Antiquities in 1857, he started a collection which in 1902 was housed in the newly opened museum. Illustrious Europeans and Egyptians have been the directors of this, the world's greatest collection of Egyptian antiquities, only a fraction of which can be displayed through lack of space.

149. If it is the day for school visits to the Egyptian Museum, you may find it hard to get a glimpse of King Tut's golden sarcophagus, one of its main attractions.

150. Thebes West, Valley of the Kings, tomb of Horemheb. The Pharaoh is depicted with Ptah, the chief god of Memphis, the first capital of Egypt. Ptah is usually shown wearing a close-fitting cap and the squared-off royal beard, as here, instead of the braided, curved beard of a god.

151. Thebes West, Valley of the Queens,
tomb of Prince Amenherkopshef, son of
Ramesses III. The beautiful wall paintings
of this rock-tunnel tomb show the Pharaoh
presenting his son to all the gods in turn.
Here, Ramesses III salutes Anubis, the
underworld god, represented with a jackal's
head.

152. Thebes, Valley of the Kings, tomb of
Horemheb of the Eighteenth Dynasty, who
ruled shortly after Tutankhamon. The
Pharaoh is in the company of Horus, the sun
god and falcon-headed son of Isis and Osiris.

153. Valley of the Kings, tomb of Horemheb.
The ruler stands between Horus and Hathor,
the mother goddess, who is often portrayed,
as here, with the sun disk and a cow's horns
on her head.

154. Abydos, temple of Sety (Sethos) I. The ubiquitous Ramesses II, wearing the crown of Lower Egypt, is greeted by Amon-Ra. The reliefs of the Abydos temple are among the finest in Egyptian art.

155. Abydos. After over three millennia, the faded colours still cling to this relief of Ramesses II, who completed the temple of Sety I, his father.

156. Priests of Amon in procession. The Opet festival lasted 24 days, starting during the second month of the annual flood. At this time, Amon's boats were taken in procession from Karnak to Luxor and back again.

157. Abd el-Qurna, Tombs of the Nobles, Thebes West. A wall painting in the tomb of Sennefer, Prince of the Southern City (i.e. Mayor of Thebes), who was in charge of the Granary and of the Stables of Amon in the reign of Amenophis (Amenhotep) II of the Eighteenth Dynasty (c. 1400 B.C.).

158. Abd el-Qurna, Tombs of the Nobles, Thebes West.Prince Sennefer and his wife, Senet-nofret, are shown here as a happy couple in their youth.The many splendid wall paintings in the Qurna tombs provide a wealth of information on everyday life.

159. The artists, masons and other craftsmen who created the wonders of Thebes had their own village at Deir el-Medina, established by Amenophis I of the Eighteenth Dynasty, the first ruler to keep the royal tomb separate from the temple of the dead.Their tombs are modest compared with those in the Valley of the Kings, but decorated with superb wall paintings depicting middle-class life in those times. This is from the tomb of Sennedjen, seen with his wife in the presence of the gods.

family. A slave girl might also become the master's concubine; whether this was quite so morally sound is another matter, but once she had borne him a child, she would often be granted her freedom. Then, as she was now emancipated, he would be likely to take her as a wife, since the moral code decreed that a free woman must not be a concubine!

In their general social interchange, the Egyptians have always been noted for their politeness of manner. Lane ascribes this to their religious background:

'The Muslims are extremely formal and regular in their social manners, though generally very easy in their demeanour and free in their conversation. Several of their most common usages are founded upon precepts of their religion, and distinguish them in society from all other people. Among these is their custom of greeting each other with a salutation of "Peace be on you!" to which the proper and general reply is, "On you be peace, and the mercy of God, and his blessing!" This salutation is never to be addressed by a Muslim to a person whom he knows to be of another religion, nor vice versa.'

Transport

Donkeys and camels, for centuries the chief means of transport, still play an important role in Egypt, even though roads are now swamped by cars and lorries, many in a dubious state of repair. Occasionally one will see a curious combination of old and new, such as an open lorry laden with kneeling camels gazing superciliously over the side. 'Asses are most generally used for riding through the narrow and crowded streets of Cairo, and there are many for hire: the usual pace is an easy amble. Egypt has long been famed for its excellent asses, which are, in general, larger than those of our country, and very superior to the latter in every respect,' proclaims Lane.

The notion of walking for reasons of health is a modern one, and in Egypt, in common with other Mediterranean countries, it was positively damaging to one's status to be caught walking out of doors: 'If he can conveniently afford to keep a horse, mule, or ass, or to hire an ass, the Egyptian is seldom seen walking far beyond the threshold of his own house,' Lane continues. Traditional methods of clearing a passage through the crowds when mounted may well account for the driving habits that prevail in Cairo today, where it is every man for himself:

'The horseman is preceded by a servant, or by two servants, to clear the way; and for the same purpose, a servant generally runs beside or behind the ass, or sometimes before, calling out to the passengers to move out of the way to the right or left, or to take care of their backs, faces, sides, feet or heels. The rider, however, must be vigilant, and not trust merely to this servant, or he may be thrown down by the wide load of a camel, which accident, indeed, is sometimes unavoidable in the more narrow and crowded streets.'

Usually the rider would arrive jostled, splashed by the water bottles and jars of oil he had bumped into along the way, with his mouth and eyes full of dust, but fundamentally none the worse for wear.

In considering Egyptian transport, the boat must not be forgotten. There have been boats on the Nile since time immemorial, and many varieties and sizes have been developed to ferry people and cargo along the river. The most common small boat seen today is the *felucca*, a traditional craft with slender white sails, often hired by the visitor to reach one of the Nile islands, or to take a short trip down the river. Victorian visitors had

160. The golden mask of King Tut', inlaid with lapis lazuli, one of the greatest treasures of the Egyptian Museum of Cairo. The young Pharaoh died in c. 1350 B.C. at the age of eighteen. The treasure of Tutankhamon, found almost intact in his tomb in the Valley of the Kings in 1922, has made him one of the best-known figures in ancient Egyptian history, in which he played a very minor role.

233

grander notions for their cruises, and sometimes chartered a dahabiya, a superior form of sailing boat which could sleep up to ten people. Those with less money could try for a *cangia*, which was slightly smaller, in which to make their voyage. Barges are used to carry cargo; today they are large, iron-hulled boats, with space enough for several crew members to live and work together during long trips.

Religion

Religion underpins Egyptian society, and has given its culture stability and endurance even through times of political upheaval. Followers of Islam have formed the bulk of the population since the early conversion campaigns of the Arab conquerors, but the Copts still represent a sizeable minority, perhaps about ten to fifteen per cent today — official figures vary. Egyptians are Sunni Muslims, members of the ruling orthodox sect of Islam, and, as much of what could be said about the practice of Islam in Egypt would apply equally to other Islamic and Arabic countries, a brief account will suffice here. The principles of the Muslim faith rest on two great tenets which are: there is no God but God, and Mohammed is his Prophet. Islam recognizes Judaism and Christianity, but considers Mohammed to be the last and greatest of a long line of prophets that includes Moses and Jesus. After him there will come no other.

The activity of prayer is most important to a Muslim, who is expected to pray five times each twenty-four hours. These prayers can be offered at home, or in the mosque, the official holy place of worship, or indeed wherever the believer happens to be at the appointed hour. The call to prayer from the minaret (tower) of a mosque, given by the muezzin, is a familiar sound to anyone who has visited an Islamic country, and is often today amplified by loudspeakers. The worshipper performs ritual ablutions, and then faces Mecca to recite the prescribed form of prayer with its accompanying gestures.

The life of the mosque is at its peak at midday prayers on a Friday, the holy day of the week. A mosque, like a Christian church, may be built on a grand or a small scale. The traditional Egyptian mosque is generally built of stone, its exterior walls simply decorated with alternate bands of red and white, and its interior possibly including an integral courtyard with a fountain, as well as the area set aside for prayer. This is furnished with a *mimbar*, or pulpit, and a platform known as the *dikkeh* where a copy of the Koran is kept to be read to the congregation. Islam has no priests as such, although religious training permits a man to become a preacher, an imam. An imam usually has another job as well, since the salary for his post is very small. Shoes must be removed before entering the mosque, and worshippers kneel on the floor to pray, which is covered with rugs or matting. Only the men pray in the main hall of the mosque; in Islamic countries women are encouraged to be modest and secluded, and therefore pray in a separate area of the mosque, or privately at home.

Islam lays down a strict code of practice for its followers to live by. In the previous eras in Egypt, this extended to the operation of the *sharia*, the religious courts which decided cases of law, but these were finally abolished by the republican government in 1955. All social mores are heavily influenced by the code, however; duties and prohibitions are laid down so that, as we have seen, eating pork and drinking alcohol are prohibited, and so are gambling and usury.

Strictly speaking, the portrayal of humans and living creatures is also forbidden, hence the development of beautiful abstract art to be found on

Arabic tiles and wall paintings. Photography can fall into this category, so that in rural areas the visitor may find the local men reluctant to allow their women to be snapped. Pilgrimage to Mecca is encouraged, and when travelling through Egypt the tourist may notice houses decorated with vivid pictures, portraying in animated sequence how its owner arrived at Mecca — a donkey, a bus or a plane, for instance, plus the sights he saw while there, all painted in simple colourful style along the whitewashed walls.

When a Muslim dies, Islamic practice requires only a simple funeral, with a reading from the Koran, before the body, wrapped in cloth, is placed in the family tomb. Egypt is renowned for its cult of the dead, however, and has retained a preference for large-scale funerals, with crowds of mourners who may be entertained in large tents erected for the occasion, decorated with coloured appliqué and furnished with carpets and gilt chairs. In Cairo,

Edward Lane: Men of the middle and higher classes.

the cemetery known as the City of the Dead contains miniature houses to shelter the deceased. Nowadays, it is inhabited as much by the living as the dead, providing a refuge for up to a million squatters.

Religious Festivals

Many religious festivals have traditionally been celebrated in Egypt, such as the day of Mohammed's ascension, and the birthday of saints and of relatives of the Prophet. Islam is governed by a lunar calendar, and thus its festivals occur at different times from year to year. The twelve lunar months form a cycle that repeats every nineteen years approximately in terms of the solar year; they are called *Moharram, Safar, Rabeea el-Owwal, Rabeea el-Tanee, Gumad el-Owwal, Gumal el-Tanee, Regeb, Shaaban, Ramadan, Showwal, Zu-el-Kaadeh (or el-Kaadeh), Zu-el-Heggeh (or el-Heggeh).* Of these, *Ramadan*, the time of the great fast, is the best known to non-Muslims.

Ramadan begins when the slender crescent of the new moon is sighted. The night when it is expected is known as *Leylet er-Rooyeh*, the night of observation, and the custom once was to send out a few observers into the desert, where the sky is clearer, to watch for its appearance. For the whole month following, Muslims must fast from sunrise to sunset, taking neither food nor drink during daylight hours — a hard test indeed, particularly in summer when the days are longer. Only those who are ill, pregnant, or too young to fast are allowed a special dispensation. Traditionally, smoking is also prohibited, as is the smelling of perfumes, the indulgence of worldly pleasures, and even the deliberate swallowing of one's own spittle. The end of *Ramadan*, also heralded by the sight of the new moon, is a time of great feasting; a special kind of cake is eaten, rather like Scottish shortbread. Everyone is expected to wear new clothes, and social visits are made, so that buses and trains are crowded with people en route to see their friends and relations.

Moharram, the first month of the year, is eminently blessed to the Egyptian Sunni Muslims, as it marks the emergence of the Sunnis as the dominant sect, a triumph over the rival Shi'ites. In Egypt during *Moharram* no marriages are contracted, and rituals are carried out to protect against the evil eye; alms are given on the tenth day, and in theory the Islamic tax should also be paid then, though this may be honoured more in the breach than in the observance.

During the third month the birth of the Prophet is celebrated. In times gone by a huge thanksgiving took place on the shores of lake Birket el-Ezbekiyah, but this had already dried up and disappeared by the time Lane was engaged in recording the country's customs. Tents were erected, and people joined in games, listened to recitations and enjoyed the performances of clowns and conjurors. Another visitor to Egypt, J.P. Seddon, found himself in the thick of celebrations given by the Saadeeyeh dervishes, one of the mystical sects of Islam, for the Prophet's birthday. On this occasion, however, the jugglers and snake-charmers were followed by gruelling displays during which the dervishes stabbed themselves with skewers, lay down on iron spikes, and tore at the snakes with their teeth, all in a state of religious ecstasy.

Lane found another festival still very much alive in Cairo, marking the birthday of the saint el-Hoseyn, and held on a Tuesday during the fourth month of the year, *Rabeea el-Tanee*. The festivities spilt out from around the mosque dedicated to the holy man, with shops staying open late at night, and processions, music-making and other entertainment carrying on until the

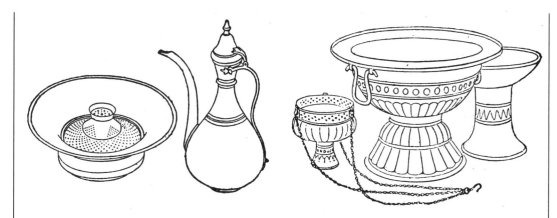

dawn. Another visitor to Egypt, the anthropologist Margaret Murray, was present at the traditional festival of the High Nile, an important occasion dating back thousands of years, now absorbed by Islam and named *Nau-ruz-Allah*, the New Year of God. The coming of the annual flood, heralded by the star Sirius was — until the building of the great Aswan Dam — one of the most significant dates in the calendar. It was regularly celebrated by letting off firecrackers and guns, and the ruling monarch would cut open an irrigation canal to allow the new waters to flow through.

The Coptic Church

The Copts represent an ancient form of Christianity and one of the last links with pre-Arabic Egypt. Many of the old Egyptian myths were absorbed into their teachings, so that Isis and her son Horus became the Virgin Mary and the infant Jesus, and the victory of Horus over the evildoer, Seth, translated into the story of St George killing the dragon. The ankh, or cross of life, thus became the cross of the crucifixion. These influences can be seen in Coptic art, and some of the old Coptic basilicas, such as those at Hermopolis Magna and Abu Mena, are based upon the hypostyle halls of the ancient Egyptian temples.

The Copts revere all the places which the Holy Family are said to have visited on their flight into Egypt. A monastery at Deir el-Muharraq on the Nile just north of Asyut marks the southernmost point of the journey: the chapel there is believed to stand on the exact spot where Mary made and lit a fire. A very old tree near Cairo is reputed to be the same one which sheltered her from the scorching sun.

The Church is headed by the Patriarch of Alexandria, and consists of various orders of clergy, who are mostly allowed to marry. The old monastic tradition continues to a limited extent with a few communities of monks and nuns living in houses such as that of St Anthony's, on the Gulf of Suez. There is little hostility between Muslims and Copts. These Egyptian Christians place a high value on education, their studies qualifying them for important positions in society: they are often found holding key posts in engineering, education and business.

Copts have their own feast days, and also various periods of fasting. The chief of these, known as the *es-Som el-Kebeer*, traditionally lasted for fifty-five days, during which only bread and pulses were allowed as food. The Coptic calendar is different from both the Islamic and the Western or Roman calendar, and is judged to begin from the era of Diocletian in A.D. 248. Each year starts on about 10 September, and contains twelve months, known, in order, as *Toot, Babeh, Hatoor, Kiyahk, Toobeh, Ansheer, Barmahat, Barmoodeh, Beshens, Ba-ooneh, Ebeeb* and *Misra*. This leaves a short space which is filled with five or six intercalary days, known as the *Eiyam en-Nesee.*

Life Today

Education

Elementary education has been compulsory since 1925, and secondary education free of charge since 1950. But the ideal of education for all is still some way off, for even official figures admit that only three-quarters of Egypt's children ever go to school, and only half of the population can read and write. A programme of state education was first instituted in the nineteenth century, but it has not been an easy scheme to implement. One of the major problems was, and still is, a lack of adequate resources: at the beginning of the Nasser era, for example, the elementary schools could only take a third of the children who should have been attending, even though efforts had been made to provide more schools, both through constructing new buildings and converting old ones. Many sleepy old mansions were now alive with the sound of children's voices, at work in class, at play in the gardens outside. Many more teachers had been trained, but it was still not enough.

Previously, Egypt was not short of schools, but they were of a totally different type. In the traditional way, children would normally attend a *kuttab*, a local school attached to the mosque, where for a very small fee they would be taught to read and write, and to study the Koran. Other schools which had sprung up, largely during the nineteenth century, all embodied different outlooks: early state schools, for example, were based on a military education, and there were also British, American and French schools, plus schools founded with a specific religious outlook — Scottish Calvinist, Italian Catholic, Greek Orthodox and, of course, Coptic.

The government has now established a more integrated education system. It is also more relevant to today's society, and to Egypt's position in the world, taking account both of national interests, and of needs for up-to-date technological training. Teacher training has been radically improved and standard textbooks revised; they are now all written in Arabic (many were published in other languages before), and care is taken that subjects such as history and geography are explained from an Egyptian viewpoint rather than carrying a colonial bias. Foreign educational establishments still exist, but they are legally obliged to teach Arabic, Islamic history and religious instruction to their Muslim students. The British Institute and the American University in Cairo continue to function, but are tolerated chiefly because they provide badly-needed tuition in the English language. Old traditions have not been entirely eradicated: in Cairo, the el-Azhar University, one of the oldest Islamic universities in the world, still opens its doors to students who pour in from more than thirty Islamic countries.

Provision for university education has increased, and the number of universities accepting students grew from four in 1952 to twelve in 1982. In 1956 technical education was reorganized at secondary and higher levels, and institutes have since been founded which specialize in the technology of cotton, petroleum and electronics. The policy of providing higher education at local level was designed to take pressure off Cairo and Alexandria, but nevertheless the more popular faculties there are still crowded out. One reason for this is the sizeable intake of foreign students from Asia and other parts of Africa, which adds to the pressure on the limited facilities. About one per cent of the Egyptian population enter university today, and there is a grants system in operation to fund their studies. In fact, every Egyptian whose grades are adequate is entitled to carry on his or her education from secondary school right through to a doctorate, if so desired.

Another reason for the growing popularity of university education is the well-meaning, but over-optimistic promise by Nasser that every graduate would be offered a job with the government. This, alas, has proved impossible to fulfil. Rather than risk the outcry that would be caused by revoking it, the government has now adopted delaying tactics, and there is a mandatory three-year period between graduation and the pledge of a job offer. This way it is hoped that many of the graduates will find themselves work elsewhere before the three years are up; additionally, women must serve a year in a social welfare agency, and men a year or two in the army before they are eligible to be considered. The popular belief of *el-shahada silah*, 'a certificate is a weapon', is not restricted to graduates, but many highly-educated youngsters find that it is not only hard to find employment, but that the kind of work for which they have been schooled brings in very little money. A biologist in a government post, for instance, can scarcely feed his family on the salary he earns, and is likely to supplement his income with more lucrative work such as taxi-driving.

Co-education is nowadays common in Egypt, though not universal. Most primary schools are mixed, but secondary schools are usually single sex. In theory universities are mixed, but with the growth of Islamic fundamentalism, segregation of the sexes has become more common again. The proportion of men and women entering university is equal however, or even tipped slightly in favour of the women.

The Position of Women

'With one sweep the 1952 Revolution took away all sexual discrimination in education and professional opportunities... As feudal wealth was eliminated and free education became available for all citizens, girls increasingly took advantage of all the educational opportunities. Furthermore, their parents began to encourage them.'

This is, at any rate, the official view, but traditional values, which restrict women to the home and family, have by no means died out, especially in the country. (Further official views and indeed much valuable information can be gleaned from the government booklet entitled *Modern Egypt*, which is published at regular intervals, giving an up-to-date survey

Edward Lane: Postures of prayer.

of Egyptian economy and society. However, it should be always borne in mind that this, and any related official press bulletins — both of which have proved helpful in compiling information for this chapter — may represent the state of Egypt as the government would like it to be, rather than as it actually is.)

It is certainly true that women have reached high positions in society: there are women professors in all branches of learning at Egyptian universities, and there are practising women doctors, scientists, lawyers and business managers. Three women have held the post of minister for social affairs, and various female under-secretaries are to be found in government ministries. The drive towards female emancipation did not begin with the revolution, for the Egyptian Feminist Union was founded by Hoda Sharawi as long ago as 1923. This was followed by the first Congress of Arab Women held in Cairo in 1938, which demanded the admission of women to university, and better working conditions for women in general. Today, state benefits are available to both sexes; there are retirement pensions for working women, and a wife has the right to claim a husband's pension if he dies before her. Traditional Islamic law is very fair to women in matters of property, and a woman's rights to retain her own property, to go into business and buy, sell or rent have always been exactly the same as those of a man.

Health and Welfare

Modern Egyptian medicine is as advanced as that of any European nation, but suffers from staff shortages and lack of adequate organization. Health care is available free, but, like their European counterparts, Egyptians who can afford to may often pay to ensure speedy treatment or a private hospital room.

Two diseases in particular have been the scourge of rural areas. The first is bilharzia, a potentially fatal, parasitic disease which enters the blood stream through breaks in the skin. It is still prevalent even though drugs have been developed to fight the disease, and great efforts made to eliminate its carriers, in particular a type of water snail: breeding areas have been treated with chemicals, and some canals lined with concrete to keep it at bay. With this illness, as with other health problems in Egypt, education is half the battle; if local people could be persuaded not to drink from the canal, or to use it as a toilet, bilharzia and various other diseases would cease to be a problem. Clean piped drinking water, as mentioned in the last chapter, is available just about everywhere in Egypt now.

The second widespread endemic disease, trachoma, has been more successfully brought under control. It is carried by flies, and is usually contracted by allowing flies to crawl over the face and eyelids. A current and effective information campaign spelling out the dangers of this, and encouraging people to bring in any infected children promptly for treatment, has considerably reduced the incidence of the disease.

Clinics that deal with such problems are now widespread. Families in rural areas need not be cut off from medical treatment, for there is likely to be a local clinic nearby, and child welfare, general health, and maternity check-up services are readily available. There are also plenty of family planning centres, but wooing customers to them is a hard job. It is still a matter of masculine pride to sire several children, and a man with only one or two children is likely to be considered well-nigh impotent! Women, for their part, regard childbearing as a way of securing the marriage in a country where divorce by the husband is easy, and childlessness looked upon as one of the greatest misfortunes.

163. Alexandria, the island of Pharos, today only a pier of the Eastern Harbour. The fort of Sultan Qayt-Bay stands on the foundations of the celebrated lighthouse, built in the third century B.C. and destroyed by an earthquake in the fourteenth century.

164. Alexandria (el-Iskandariya to the Egyptians) was founded by Alexander the Great in 332 B.C., though he never saw the city, to which his body was brought back for burial. Today the second largest city and main port of Egypt, it has a much more European air than the capital.

165. Cairo, the Bab el-Nasr or Victory Gate, at the north-east end of the old Islamic city of el-Qahira. This is the best preserved of the three surviving gates of the original 60 which formed part of the fortifications raised in the eleventh century.

166. *The city of el-Fayyum: a modern mosque, modelled on the medieval Mamluk mosques of Cairo, and in the foreground, the Bahr el-Yussuf. Through its branches it brings fertility to the Fayyum, drawing its water from the Nile via the Ibrahimiya Canal. The Joseph of its name refers in fact to the great twelfth-century ruler Saladin, but he is thought only to have repaired a waterway of pharaonic origin.*

167. *The city of el-Fayyum (Faiyum), centre of the green Fayyum depression, intersected by the ancient waterway known as the Bahr el-Yussuf or River of Joseph. The intensively cultivated Fayyum has over two million inhabitants.*

168. *Cairo Citadel, the mosque of Mohammed (Mehmet) Ali Pasha, a city landmark. Built between 1830 and 1857 by a Turkish architect, it was modelled on the Yeni mosque in Istanbul.*

169. *Alexandria, the Abu el-Abbas mosque, the largest and most beautiful in the city.It was raised in the late eighteenth century over the tomb of a revered scholar from Mercia (Spain), who lived in Alexandria in the thirteenth century.*

170. View of Hurghada on the Red Sea, a town that has developed in recent years into a major holiday resort on this coast.

171. Aswan. On the left bank of the Nile, opposite Elephantine Island, stands the great fortress-like mausoleum of Aga Khan III, the immensely wealthy leader of the Shi'ite sect of Ismailites.Before his death in 1957, he requested that this sandstone and pink granite funerary monument be raised here, on his favourite spot, which commands a beautiful view.

172. A mosque in Aswan, Egypt's southernmost city of any size. Since ancient times it has been the gateway to Nubia and Central Africa.The quarries of this area provided the stone for many of the great monuments.A few miles south is the Aswan High Dam, 364 ft high and three miles long, opened in 1971.

173. Cairo, worshippers inside the mosque of el-Muayad Sheik. Of the original building, raised at the beginning of the fifteenth century by a Mamluk ruler, little remains except the prayer room, lavishly decorated with fine materials, especially the mihrab wall with seven niches.

174. *'Eat what you please, wear what pleases others,' runs the old Arab proverb.*

175. *New settlements and palm plantations in the Inner Oases enjoy the benefits of artesian wells.The New Valley project is a scheme aimed at increasing the area of cultivable land in the Western Desert. (pp. 254-255)*

Inoculation against the worst diseases is now widely available, and can be made compulsory in the case of an epidemic. The government claims that cholera, smallpox and malaria have been eradicated, but in the case of malaria, at least, this does not seem to be strictly true, for posters warning people of its existence are still displayed. A new disease is now becoming rife in the cities: diabetes. This may be triggered by urban habits of eating too much sugar; Egyptians are very fond of sweets and sugary foods, and those who live in the cities tend to have both the money and the opportunity to indulge to excess. Liver complaints are also on the increase, caused by eating too much rich food with a high percentage of fat, which is hard to burn off in a hot climate.

Egypt is, in effect, a welfare state, half British, half communist in character — reflecting the major influences upon the country's development this century. Certain essential food stuffs are subsidized by the state, including bread, rice, dried beans, lentils and cooking oil. Fruit and vegetables are price-controlled, according to the state of the harvest, and there are co-operative stores where products such as these must be sold at reasonable prices, usually lower than those of their private competitors. Another area to benefit from public subsidy is transport, where fares are kept low. Schools, as we have seen, provide free education, in addition to which any school clothing required is also issued without charge, both to pupils and to teachers.

Housing and the Environment

Home life is important to the Egyptian, and home ownership a goal which is given high priority. The care that is lavished on the home may not immediately be apparent, for, as in other Mediterranean countries, there is often a sharp contrast between the exterior and the interior of a house. Outside, all the casual passer-by sees may be broken fences, a neglected garden, and dirty walls. Inside, everything may be spotlessly clean and tidy, with rooms furnished to the highest standard that the family can afford.

Many city dwellers live in apartments, usually consisting of a living room, dining room, one or two bedrooms, kitchen and bathroom. The entrance hall is often spacious and can be adapted for use as a dining area or, if the family needs it, another bedroom. A balcony is a common, much-enjoyed feature, making a pleasant place to sit out on a summer's evening. Traditional furniture is still generally preferred to modern design, with sofas, chairs, and ornate occasional tables of carved and gilded wood; the visitor may often glimpse examples of these sitting in a carpenter's workshop in Cairo, awaiting despatch to their proud new owners. In middle-class urban homes ornaments are admired and collected — small figurines, vases and pictures decorate the walls and sideboard — and domestic technology much appreciated. Few homes are without a refrigerator, essential in such a hot climate, and many possess a dishwasher, a washing machine, and, of course, a television. Some flats have air conditioning installed to make life more tolerable in the summer heat.

In rural communities, such luxuries are scarce, and the closest the typical peasant family comes to air conditioning is an open door to let in the faithful evening breeze from the Nile! Country homes may be cleaner on the outside than their urban counterparts and more spartan on the inside. Such houses are traditionally built of unbaked mud bricks, fashioned by hand on the river bank, but now any new building must use bricks made of sand in order to conserve the banks and the rich humus of the Nile Valley. The houses are heated in winter by burning dried cotton bushes, and fuel for

176. Bird's eye view of a village near Luxor in Upper Egypt, a typical jigsaw of dilapidated, new and unfinished dwellings with the mosque as the focal point of the settlement.

cooking in clay ovens is provided from lumps of dried cow dung mixed with straw. In the simplest type of house, a platform runs across the room to act as seating, and the oven may be situated underneath it. In houses to the south of the country, bread ovens may be portable so that they can be taken outside to do the baking.

Everyone in Egypt, rich and poor, urban and rural, has a problem with dust. Dust is everywhere, and at certain times of year it blows through every chink and cranny, leaving a fine coating over the entire house and its contents. Most homes are cleaned daily, but the dust still comes in, however securely doors and windows are fastened, and however affluent or well-kept the house may be.

Rents in Egypt are controlled, and kept to a reasonable level, but new homes nevertheless often carry rents which are too high for the majority to afford. Additionally, sizeable deposits may be demanded by the landlord, and those who would prefer to buy a house or apartment find prices way beyond their means. The government has stepped in to help by offering mortgages to those buying a flat for the first time, and by building low-priced housing units, for sale only to first-time buyers and those with young families. Unfortunately, examples that the author has seen look shabby and are obviously of poor quality, so that one can only hope the standards will improve. President Mubarak is, after all, noted for his efficient and far-sighted housing policy; already new towns are springing up around Cairo to meet the desperate shortage of accommodation, settlements known as Sadat City, Salam City, 15th of May City, and 6th of October City.

Utopian schemes for housing the needy do not always go according to plan. Even before the 1952 Revolution, a scheme had been drawn up to build an ideal village in a 'neo-Egyptian' style, to be known as New Qurna. Here the inhabitants of the existing Qurna were to be resettled, and enjoy excellent educational, medical, and community facilities. However, the project first ran into difficulties with cut-backs in government funding, so that the village that was eventually built did not conform to the original vision, although it did have an exhibition hall, a community hall, a covered market and a theatre. But the real problem was that nobody wanted to live in it. The inhabitants of Qurna preferred to stay put, claiming that the red baked bricks used in the construction of the houses would not give them such good insulation as their traditional mud brick homes. While this may be true, it was only an excuse; the villagers had quite another reason for their refusal. For centuries, the inhabitants of Thebes have supplemented their income by grave robbing. If a house is built on top of a tomb, then there is nothing to prevent its occupants from excavating their 'cellar' and disposing of the treasures they may find there. The planners knew this full well, and the villagers were not taken in by the apparent gesture of concern for their welfare; nothing could persuade them to move and give up this, their lucrative and 'traditional' source of income.

Since the New Qurna experiment, architects have largely given up their dreams of fine architecture for the masses, and now tend to build in the anonymous, dreary style common to the urban areas of poorer countries everywhere. In Cairo, a jumble of faceless modern buildings, some of them half-finished, dominates the city. When the Russians were dismissed by President Sadat, they simply left off the construction work they were engaged in, in some cases taking away with them vital plans, such as the plumbing schemes.

Little is left of medieval Cairo, and the city is strained to bursting point. The traffic is of phenomenal density, a constant dusty stream of battered vehicles, belching out black smoke, hooting, forcing their way ever onwards. Road markings and traffic lights are totally ignored, and pedestrians are often obliged to clamber over the cars to cross the road. Public transport is little better, for buses are not only packed inside, but outside as well, with a crowd of men and boys hanging on from anything that will give them a handhold.

Whatever good intentions the government possesses, it is a hard task indeed to provide enough housing for such a rapidly growing population. Egypt had 46 million inhabitants in 1948, and by the year 2000 the population is expected to reach 70 million. Egyptian cities do retain something of their original character, including a touch of nineteenth-century grandeur, but they have been forcibly overtaken by the demands of the twentieth century, unable to absorb the less desirable elements of modern life with any grace at all.

The Economy

When considering the Egyptian economy, agriculture and industry can be included together, for they are vitally interconnected. Raw materials produced by the land, including oil and minerals, are largely processed within the country. Even water is an economic commodity whose distribution must be carefully controlled. For present purposes, all the major elements of the economy will therefore be described with little distinction made between natural and manufactured products.

The chief crop of Egypt is cotton, famous throughout the world for its excellent quality. Cotton can be picked twice a year, resulting in a prime and a second-quality harvest. Its production is pleasing to the eye, creating beautiful green fields among the palm trees, yellow with flowers in season. Its cultivation demands hard labour, however, and, because it depletes the soil, a great quantity of fertilizer must be used to ensure good enough crops. Introduced to Egypt during Mehmet Ali's reign, after the construction of the Delta Barrage, cotton now occupies about a quarter of the cultivated area in the Delta region.

Originally, Egyptian cotton was exported to be spun and woven into cloth abroad. But when this became uneconomic, and mills in the great spinning centres like Manchester closed down, Egypt had to set up its own factories for cotton manufacture. Cotton spinning demands certain climatic conditions — the Lancashire area of England was ideal because it was very damp — and so a suitable alternative location had to be found. Experts finally settled upon the middle region of the Delta, where Mahalla has since become a focus of spinning and weaving, growing from small beginnings to become a major centre for the industry. All grades of material are produced at the Mahalla mills, synthetic as well as cotton, ranging from heavy-duty cotton to fine, delicate material, suitable for ladies' evening wear.

Egyptian factories do not always have the best of modern equipment; indeed, ever since the first attempts to introduce industry last century, the country has had to make do with a great many European cast-offs. Machinery is therefore often obsolete, in poor repair and prone to break down. Egyptian mechanics have developed a high degree of ingenuity in their work, and specialize in keeping moribund machines going for as long as possible. Opportunities for industrial training are provided by technical colleges, of which there are some 350 in Egypt, but as these cannot cope with the demand, a number of students go abroad to study.

Factories have also been built to produce fertilizers, which are needed in far greater quantities since the opening of the High Dam at Aswan. Both the fertilizer plants and cotton mills, and also the sugar refineries are

Water has always been a precious commodity in Egypt.

responsible for terrible pollution, and pose a real health risk to their employees. Another industry which blights the environment is steel production, seen at its worst in the town of Helwan, some twelve miles south of Cairo.

Helwan was once an attractive holiday resort, dating back many centuries: the governor of Egypt, Abd el-Aziz Ibn Marun, came there to take the waters for his health in 968. In the nineteenth century, a Moorish bath house was built, along with large hotels, a casino, and even a Japanese garden. But since the 1950s this has been overshadowed by the development of a vast steel plant, with foundries and manufacturing units that have all but taken over the town. The old spa building is surrounded by blocks of high-rise flats, built of dull grey concrete, many unfinished; streets are obstructed by heaps of rubble and refuse, against a backdrop of chimneys belching out gigantic clouds of smoke. As the local people say: 'Helwan is no longer a place to go for a picnic.'

Helwan's main product was iron rods, used in reinforced concrete construction, but now other, more sophisticated goods are also manufactured there: domestic appliances, spare parts for cars, and electronic equipment. Barges from Aswan bring iron ore to the city, and manganese, zinc, copper and lead are sent over from the Western and Eastern Deserts. Coal, the original fuel used, was replaced by electricity after the building of the High Dam. This in turn has now been supplanted by gas piped in from the oil fields.

Egypt's petroleum industry is still only partially developed. The main areas where oil has been found are the Western Desert, the Sinai Peninsula, and, most importantly, the Gulf of Suez, where 90 per cent of oil production comes from at present. Exports are on the way up: in 1975 oil formed nearly 10 per cent of total exports, but in 1986 this had risen to over half. The oil wells in the Sinai area, developed by the Israelis when the land was under their control, are the least productive. The Western Desert, on the other hand, although not yet fully investigated, has raised considerable hopes as to its prospects. In the Gulf of Suez, off shore drilling has tapped

Edward Lane: Musicians.

large reservoirs of oil, and major oil-producing companies, including Mobil and Esso, are now engaged in operations in the area. In 1967 the Gupco company was formed, a joint venture between Pan American Oil and the Egyptian government, and a similar enterprise, Suco, the Suez Oil Company, now pumps ashore some 30,000 barrels of oil a day.

Life on the oil rigs is said to be dull, but well-paid — a similar tale the world over. The oil industry is structured so as to protect national interests; Egyptian workers are in the majority on the rigs, and profits are strictly controlled, foreign companies retaining only 25 to 30 per cent, with the rest going to the Egyptian government. Elsewhere in the country, foreign investment is welcomed as long as it will really benefit the Egyptian economy.

Active economic planning has proved to be a necessity. Internally, the government has made serious attempts at good housekeeping, taking financial advice from international experts, imposing import controls, spending foreign aid prudently, and attempting, at least, to control tax evasion. To improve job opportunities locally, it has made a commitment to decentralize industry, and house much of it in new cities throughout the country.

The government is also concerned to raise agricultural standards. The ministry of agriculture has set up a network of experts who visit rural areas to give advice on fertilizers, pesticides, crops and seeds. The public Bank of Agriculture, a division of the Central Bank of Egypt, helps to arrange loans for land improvement to farmers, most of whom today are *fellahin* working on smallholdings allocated to them during the Nasser era. The days of large-scale landowners are over: the 'middle-class' farmer owning more than the average amount of land is likely to live and work on it himself, rather than remaining an absentee landlord, as was so often the case in the past.

Other crops apart from cotton include *berseem*, or medic grass, which is widely grown to provide animal fodder and a natural fertilizer for the soil. Rice is the chief crop of the Fayyum, but is grown too in parts of the Delta region, where maize is also harvested. In Upper Egypt crops to feed

the local population, such as millet and sorghum, take priority, as there is less land overall available for cultivation. Sugar cane is an important product of the Thebes basin, and is usually harvested in February; wines and figs grow near the north coast, olives in the Fayyum depression, and citrus fruits around Cairo. Vegetables are widely cultivated, especially in areas near cities.

Land reclamation is still proceeding, and new green fields can be seen along the road between Cairo and Alexandria, formerly arid desert. To the west of the Suez Canal, another scheme, known as the Salhiya Project, has also brought about the 'greening' of the desert, and in the Western Desert, the 'New Valley' enterprise is providing irrigation from artesian wells for the string of oases there. Water is vital in Egypt, a factor in almost any economic equation, and the source of the country's main electricity supply as well. Some 88 million cubic metres of water are available for agriculture from the Nile every year, but Egypt must share these with neighbouring Sudan. In order to safeguard the interests of both countries, a treaty lays down exactly how many gallons each of them is entitled to.

Culture and Entertainment

There is a flourishing world of the arts in Egypt, unknown as it may be to those outside the Arab world. In 1956 the government set up an official body with the rather grand title of the Higher Council for the Patronization of the Arts, Letters and Sciences, which has had a considerable influence upon cultural development. For students interested in fine arts, training is available at the Faculty of Fine Arts in Cairo, and among established artists there is a refreshing variety of outlook. Inji Aflatun, for instance, is a noted landscape painter, while Ahmed Rashidi specializes in portraits of country peasants; Salah Taher is popular for his romantic compositions based on the Nile, and Ahmed Rifaat for lively murals, predominantly red and orange, featuring horses and boats. Sculpture is also well represented, and the father of the modern school in Egypt is generally considered to be Mokhtar, whose works may be seen in the streets and parks of Cairo.

The development of Egyptian literature owes something to the rise of journalism. In most countries, journalism represents the superficial element of literary output, but in Egypt it helped to elevate standards, creating a modern form of Arabic that could express contemporary ideas. Since then, journalism has remained central to the intellectual and literary life of the country. In 1960 all newspapers in Egypt were nationalized, so that the press is now an official organ. Among the leading papers which have since been on sale are *El-Ahram* (The Pyramids), *El-Akhbar* (The News) and *El-Gymhuriya* (The Republic).

Moving on to fiction, the best-known contemporary novelist is Najib Mahfuz from Cairo, a representative of the modern school of realism, which takes an uncompromising look at Egyptian society. His work has reached a wider audience, for in 1988 he was awarded the Nobel Prize for Literature. Novels were not produced in Egypt until the 1940s, and are not the main literary genre today, although there are other well-known figures in the field, such as Ibrahim el-Manzini, and Abd el-Rahman el-Sharqawe. Short stories came to prominence earlier; the works of Mohammed Taymur, written around the time of the First World War and displaying a certain Russian influence, are the first of their kind in Arabic.

Poetry is perhaps more deeply rooted in the Arabic tradition than narrative fiction. The renaissance of Egyptian poetry began with Sami Pasha el-Barudi, who was Prime Minister for a brief spell in 1882. Barudi was

more fortunate in his literary efforts, where he was inspired by the Abbasid poets of the eighth to thirteenth centuries, and was himself the inspiration for other later poets such as Ismail Sabri, Hafiz Ibrahim and Ahmad Shawqi. Ahmad Shawqi developed his own style, a type of epic poetry with dramatic content which strongly influenced the form of subsequent films, plays and operettas. Some of his own works were adapted into musicals, including *The Death of Cleopatra*, and *The Princess of Andalusia*. As with the novel, a preference for lyrical, romantic work earlier this century eventually gave way to the demand for topical literature concerned with national and social issues; two of the leading representatives of the school of realism today are Salah Abd el-Sabur, and Ahmad Hijazi.

Artistic freedom of expression now may be under threat, though, with the resurgence of religious orthodoxy. Mahfuz, the Nobel Prize winner, has himself had one of his novels banned by the authorities, and a writer called Alaa Hamed was recently branded as 'the Egyptian Salman Rushdie' and sentenced to eight years imprisonment for a story written on the theme of Islamic paradise. His publisher was also sentenced and fined, and both men have been the target of death threats, according to Egyptian reports in December 1991.

Entering the area of the performing arts, we find that theatre became established in the nineteenth century. At first only translations of French plays were presented, but later preference was given to works by Egyptian dramatists, which today include playwrights Yusuf Idris and Nu'man Ashur. Foreign works are still acted on the Egyptian stage, with the plays of Shakespeare a perennial favourite. Not all theatre productions are serious; on the lighter side, comedies are regularly staged and draw huge crowds. Acting companies may be resident or touring; there is an Egyptian National Theatre, and grants are available locally for budding amateur theatre groups.

The cinema is even more popular. Cairo is the main centre producing films and videos for the Arab world, and Egypt has hosted an international film festival each year since 1976. Egypt has spawned a galaxy of film stars, most of them unknown outside their own country, with certain notable exceptions like Omar Sharif. Some of the best-loved faces today are those of actresses Souad Hosny, Mervat Amin and Naglaa Fathy, and ac-

178. Deir el-Bahari, Thebes West. The first pharaoh to build a temple of the dead here, in c. 2000 B.C., was Mentuhotep II of the Middle Kingdom. Much better preserved is the temple of Queen Hatshepsut, built some 550 years later. The whole area is pitted and mounded, searched and upturned, by generations of grave robbers, antiquarians and archaeologists. (pp. 266-267)

179. Deir el-Bahari, Thebes West, the great mortuary temple of Queen Hatshepsut with the ruins of the older temple of Mentuhotep II beside it. Hatshepsut's memorial fittingly commemorates the first woman ruler in history. (pp. 268-269)

tors Nour Sherif, Hussein Fahmy, Mahmoud Yassin and Ahmed Faki. Egypt has a long history of film-making, for the first feature picture was produced there as far back as 1935, with the years between 1945 and 1952 representing the peak of production, a golden age of film. The pace in Egyptian films is slower than westerners may be used to; audiences like to linger over the unfolding of the plot, and to relish all the colourful details of costume and scenery.

In almost every country in the world, television has gained a hold, and Egypt is no exception. The first Egyptian stations began transmission in 1960, and television is now ubiquitous; plenty of traditional mud brick houses in rural villages have a television set, as well as the more sophisticated homes in the cities. Viewers have been gripped by the occasional national offering, such as *The White Flag*, a humorous soap opera screened in 1989, as well as by the inevitable outpouring of serials and soaps from Europe and America. Programmes also include sports coverage, and an apparently unending footage of the President faithfully carrying out his many official duties.

Egyptian music reflects various influences. Its origins are mainly oriental, and in its classical Arabic form, it is taught at the Cairo Institute of Oriental Music. But it also includes a strong folk song tradition, which has remained popular to this day and made the name of a number of singers, the most famous of all being Om Kalsoum, a female singer who died in the 1980s. Music in the classical western tradition is not neglected; it is taught in conservatories, and regularly performed in concert. An appealing mixture of the two types of music, Arabic and western, has been developed, which is known as Franco-Arabic music and bears a resemblance to Algerian 'RAI'. Classical opera got off to a flying start in Egypt over a century ago, with the first production of Verdi's *Aida* at the Pyramids, and the building of an opera house in Cairo to celebrate the opening of the Suez Canal. The original building was destroyed by fire in 1971, and a new opera house to replace it is at present being constructed on Gazira Island.

Dance is represented in Egypt both through traditional folk dances and western forms such as classical ballet. Belly dancing, more properly known as *raqs sharqi*, is enjoying something of a revival today and its popularity has spread far beyond Egypt. In its original form, it is a very beautiful, artistic, and therapeutic form of women's dance, not the cheap form of titillation commonly found in night clubs.

As far as sport goes, football (soccer) is easily the favourite game in Egypt, the 'big match' being watched on television every Friday. When the two leading Egyptian teams, Ahli and Zamalek, play each other, the streets of Cairo empty as if by magic. There are plenty of football games at local level too, and every village or school has its own team. Swimming is also a sport that has been taken seriously in Egypt for many years; long-distance training still takes place in the Nile and one can only hope that the swimmers keep their mouths shut as they practise! Egyptian competitors do well in international swimming competitions, as indeed they do also in tennis, a more recent addition to the range of sports practised.

In this brief survey of modern Egyptian life, it can be seen that the country has taken up many of the opportunities and challenges offered by the twentieth century. It is not free from the problems that such progress also brings, especially pollution, domination by the motor car, and all the health and environmental ills that are thus created. But one lesson that Egypt does seem to have learnt from the past is how to further its national interests and promote home-grown talent. It keeps its doors open to the world, while at the same time strengthening and affirming its own identity.

180. Thebes West, the mortuary temple of Ramesses II the Great. Reduced to bare bones, the mighty ruin still impresses with its solidity and mass. It was Champollion who named the temple 'Ramesseum'. In the background, the houses of alabaster craftsmen and tomb robbers stand on the slope of Qurnet Murai.

181. The village of Sheik Abd el-Qurna, close to the Ramesseum, grew up around the tombs of the Pharaoh's high officials, which are remarkable for their wall paintings. The Ramesseum is not only a mortuary monument but also a temple dedicated to Amon-united-with-eternity.

182. The severed granite head of 'Ozymandias', nose and beard missing, stands in the dust before the Ramesseum at Thebes. The expression of Ramesses II is one of total confidence in the eternal duration of his memory. (pp. 272-273)

183. The temple of Luxor, raised by Amenophis III in the Eighteenth Dynasty and enlarged by Ramesses II in the Nineteenth. The impressive first pylon is flanked by statues of the latter ruler and one of the two obelisks he erected. The other, sent to Paris as a gift in 1836, now stands in the Place de la Concorde. (pp. 274-275)

273

184. Karnak, colonnade and sphinxes in the first courtyard of the temple of Amon, the largest temple courtyard in Egypt. When it was constructed in the Twenty-second Dynasty, it incorporated two smaller shrines that had previously stood outside the Amon temple complex.

185. Karnak, the temple of Amon. The
statue of Pinodjem, High Priest of Amon-Ra
during the Twenty-first Dynasty, towers
above the visitor in the courtyard west of the
second pylon.

186. Deir el-Bahari, a glimpse of Queen Hatshepsut's mortuary temple. Neatly — perhaps too neatly — restored by East European teams of archaeologists, it does not show its age. The whiteness of the fine limestone gallery stands out sharply against the lofty red cliffs, beyond which lies the Valley of the Kings.

187. Luxor, a colossal head of Ramesses II beside its pedestal, with its restored companion behind. Of the four colossi of the Pharaoh which guarded the pylon, two were standing and two seated.

188. *Karnak, one of the ram-headed sphinxes flanking the avenue leading from the Nile bank to the first pylon of the temple complex. This gateway, never completed, is the most recent part of the great temple of Amon. Work continued on it until the Thirtieth Dynasty.*

The Visitor in Egypt

Early Travellers

Even before the Christian era, visitors came to marvel at the monuments of Egypt, and sometimes used the stones themselves as a kind of visitor's book on which to record their impressions. The toe of the Sphinx is inscribed with a poem in ancient Greek, musing on life's transience, while a Roman lady left a poignant memento at the Great Pyramids: 'I saw the pyramids without you; sadly I shed tears there.' Ancient Egyptians themselves scribbled notes on a nobleman's house at Saqqara, admiring the edifices of their even more ancient ancestors. Warriors, monarchs and scholars travelled to Egypt to marvel at its wonders, among them Herodotus, Strabo, and the Emperor Hadrian.

Not all the sights which they enjoyed remain to us today. The Labyrinth at Hawara, for instance, one of the chief attractions for Roman tourists, was built as a mortuary temple for Amenemhat III, its layout a complex labyrinth of rooms and pillars, surmounted by a pyramid. Since those days the building has been dismantled, leaving only a few fragmentary outlines of its past glory. Sometimes historians can drawn on the accounts left by those early visitors — Herodotus in particular — to fill out details of everyday life, sacred rituals, and the appearance of ancient monuments long lost to mankind.

After the classical period, there was no real tourism in Egypt until the end of the eighteenth century. Before that, the only visitors were nomads traversing the region, or the occasional merchant or pilgrim from Europe. But gradually it was realized that a wealth of treasure remained there for the taking: first the odd papyrus or mummy was shipped home for its curiosity value, and then serious collectors began to make their killing. Some was offered in homage, such as the treasure trove presented to King Louis XIV of France by his Consul Benoît de Maille. Other eighteenth-century spoils eventually came to form major Egyptian collections in Europe, seen today in museums at Turin and Leiden, in the British Museum and the Louvre.

Not until after the Napoleonic expedition did Egypt become a country which was visited primarily for its culture. During this brief French occupation, the team of specialists who had travelled to Egypt with Napoleon plunged into a comprehensive research programme: scores of geographers, antiquarians, botanists, architects, geologists, and other experts swarmed over the Delta and the Nile Valley regions, observing, measuring, digging and deciphering. The publication of their findings helped to put Egypt back on the map; it stirred the imagination of the British, the Germans, and the Americans too. Over the following century and a half Egypt became a country which attracted not only the educated tourist, but also artists and writers, among them such well-known names as Gustave Flaubert, Edward Lear, Sir Arthur Conan Doyle, Rudyard Kipling, Vita Sackville-West and William Golding.

Flaubert began his trip in 1849, setting out on what was to be an 'oriental' adventure through Egypt and other Middle Eastern countries. He was twenty-eight at the time, with his finest work, *Madame Bovary,* still to come, and he cut a romantic figure — tall, blond, and inspired by a passion for the exotic that he found in the works of Byron and Victor Hugo, and in the stories of the Arabian Nights. He found the reality of the Egyptian desert not entirely a romantic experience. His good friend and travelling companion, Maxime du Camp, did not speak to him for two days after Flaubert raved on incessantly about lemon ices during their hot, thirsty trek! Flaubert's expedition eventually produced several novels set in Middle Eastern locations, and his correspondence from Egypt makes fine reading.

189. Karnak, granite statue of the High Priest of Amon, Pinodjem, in the temple of Amon. At, or rather, on his feet stands his wife, a lesser being and therefore much smaller.

The Growth of Archaeology

Archaeology is a comparatively recent science. Only in the last century has excavation been carried out using precise techniques to map the pattern of the past, rather than just unearthing whatever treasure could be found. In Egypt the first real archaeology was practised by the British expert William Flinders Petrie, who arrived in 1880. Napoleon's team had, of course, acted according to the best knowledge of the day, and in fact their expedition helped to unlock the mystery of hieroglyphics, which could not previously be deciphered. While investigating the Delta region in 1799, they found a black stone inscribed in three languages, its text translated from hieroglyphics into demotic Egyptian, and Greek. Here was the key which had long been sought, and together with the work of a French nobleman and Egyptologist, Jean-François Champollion, it led to a complete formulation of Egyptian grammar. The Rosetta Stone, as it is known, today resides in the British Museum, a historical landmark as well as an antiquity in its own right.

Petrie investigated many sites, including the pyramids of Hawara and el-Lahun, and recorded his findings meticulously. His work inspired the steady stream of archaeologists that poured into Egypt in the peaceful days before World War I. They practically turned the country upside-down, excavating historical sites, drawing and restoring monuments, and putting a picture of Egypt before the eyes of the world which was now perhaps less romantic, but closer to the truth. Previous generations had used their imagination rather than their investigative skills to interpret the ancient wonders; Francesco Frescobaldi in the fourteenth century thought that the Pyramids were Joseph's granaries, for instance.

Egyptian archaeology at the beginning of the twentieth century was not completely accurate. Dates were placed too far back in time, and the different periods of pharaonic rule were not yet clearly understood. Since then, modern techniques, such as radio carbon dating, have helped to give a more comprehensive picture of Egypt's history. And further important discoveries have been made, the most spectacular among them being the opening in 1922 of Tutankhamon's tomb, from which a stunning array of funerary treasures was removed. Another milestone was the moving of the great temples and stone-carved figures of Abu Simbel, which would have been flooded by the opening of the Aswan High Dam; these were relocated 600 feet above their original site by complex technological methods which included resin injections, and the use of protective dams and metal frameworks.

The Visitor Today

A stay that often lasted a whole winter season for the leisured nineteenth-century traveller is now perhaps compressed into just a week or two for today's visitor. Much can be seen and enjoyed in that time, however; many tours are accompanied by extremely knowledgeable guides, and the linear settlement pattern of Egypt along the Nile means that most sites of importance can be visited taking a straightforward route by coach, train or boat. Only a very brief review of the major sites can be given here, and for a comprehensive listing, the reader is recommended to consult the range of excellent guide books available.

The Egyptians are a welcoming and friendly nation, with a patience and sophistication born of their long history. Street traders and children

The Rosetta Stone, the key to the deciphering of Egyptian hieroglyphics.

will always pester the tourist for custom or *bakshish*, but the bantering is good-humoured. Many individuals will offer to be your guide, and it can be worthwhile to accept; rates are not expensive by Western standards, and you may be taken to places that you would not normally see, including temples which are officially closed to the public!

The Major Sites

Think of Egypt, and probably the first picture that will come to mind is of the Great Pyramids at Giza. Yet the Giza pyramids, although the best-known, are by no means the only ones that can be visited. There are about half a dozen other sites of note where pyramids in various states of preservation can be seen, including Saqqara, famous for its stepped pyramid, Lisht, Abu Roash, and Meidum, site of the remains of the oldest known pyramid in Egypt. The pyramids at Giza were erected around 2500 B.C. as funerary chambers for the rulers of the Fourth Dynasty. The largest is the pyramid of Cheops, built to a height of 490 feet, followed by the pyramids of Cephren and Mycerinus. Within the Giza complex stands the enigmatic sandstone figure of the Great Sphinx, its dating and origin still something of a mystery to archaeologists. Giza is not the peaceful desert setting most people imagine; it is almost caught up in the Cairo sprawl today, and far from tidy, but it is still a place of atmosphere and majesty, one that should not be missed on a trip to Egypt.

To see the finest collection of Egyptian antiquities, it is necessary to visit Cairo. Comments about traffic and pollution in the last chapter may have dampened the reader's enthusiasm, but although it is a crowded, noisy, dirty city, it has much to offer. It also draws together the different threads of Egyptian history: ancient Egyptian, Coptic and Islamic. This book has explored these three themes, which co-exist in Egypt today in various ways, the main way, as far as the visitor is concerned, being in the monuments and museums representing each strand of culture. The Egyptian Museum has over 100,000 objects on display, dating from the prehistoric period to the Greek era.

Here can be seen the treasures of Tutankhamon, a rich harvest of superb artistry and craftsmanship. The Coptic Museum in Cairo houses stone carvings, chiefly dating from the sixth century A.D., and exquisite textiles woven in fine linen thread. There are also old Coptic churches which can be visited, such as those of St Sergius and St George. For the Islamic influence, a visit is recommended to the Islamic Museum of Art, where exhibits from the seventh century onwards include mosaics, calligraphy, metalwork, ceramics, jewellery, furnishings, textiles and weaponry.

Among the oldest and most famous of Cairo's many mosques are those of Amr Ibn el-As, and Ibn Tulun. From the medieval period there is the Islamic university and mosque of el-Azhar, and the great Citadel, built as a stronghold for Saladin and his men in the twelfth century. Three of the medieval gates to the city still survive; there is a lively bazaar to explore — and perhaps to get lost in — and a camel market, all reminders of the traditional Egyptian way of life. There are also agreeable aspects of more recent culture, such as pleasant gardens, river walks, and interesting buildings in the Art Nouveau and Art Deco styles.

For most tours, Cairo is a starting point, although when travel to Egypt was by boat, Alexandria was the city of arrival. Alexandria is more European in flavour, a Mediterranean port and seaside resort with good bathing beaches, the once fashionable Corniche promenade, 12 miles in length, and some noted antiquities of its own. Not, alas, the celebrated library or lighthouse; of these, nothing remains. But there is a Roman theatre, some early Christian catacombs, a fifteenth-century fort, and a single column, known as Pompey's Pillar, the sole survivor of the ancient religious centre of the Serapeum. The Museum of Graeco-Roman Antiquities illustrates the multi-cultural early history of this fascinating city. Nearby lie the ruins of the city of Canopus, dating from the early centuries of the Christian era. Alexandria has also acquired a certain romantic aura in the twentieth century through the writings of Lawrence Durrell, author of the acclaimed *Alexandrian Quartet*.

Travelling southwards down the Nile brings the visitor to Luxor, and into the most significant region for temples and tombs. In Luxor itself is the great temple built by Amenophis III in honour of the divine triad of Amon, Mut, and their son Khonsu. More impressive still, however, is the temple complex at neighbouring Karnak. These two sites were once linked by an avenue of ram-headed sphinxes over one mile in length, part of which is still preserved today. Some experts estimate that Karnak is the largest temple site in the world, and today's visitor can enjoy an excellent *son et lumière* display which highlights the grandeur and drama of its history.

At Karnak each successive pharaoh built his own addition to the site, so that it is very difficult now, with some of the monuments in ruins, to understand the original lay-out. Construction of the Great Temple of Amon began in the days of the Twelfth Dynasty, for instance, but embellishments were still being made at the time of the Twenty-fifth Dynasty. One of the most impressive sights, considered to be a wonder of the world even in antiquity, is the Great Hypostyle Hall, with 134 majestic columns rising from an area equivalent to the floor space of a large European cathedral. Among the less explored, smaller monuments is an exquisite temple of Osiris, with vivid wall paintings. There is also a sacred lake at Karnak, about one hundred yards in length, and several other temples of note, including the Temple of Khonsu, the Temple of Mut, and the Temple of Ramesses III.

Crossing the Nile into the region of West Thebes, the Valley of the Kings and the Valley of the Queens can be reached. These are the most important ancient tomb sites in Egypt: over sixty tombs have been discovered in the Valley of the Kings alone. The three tombs which are probably most worth visiting are those of Ramesses VI, Sety I, and, of course, Tutankhamon. Something of the ancient mystery can still be sensed: penetrating to the heart of the tomb of Ramesses VI requires a long descent through twelve portals representing the twelve gates of death.

In the Valley of the Queens about seventy tombs have been explored, of which the tombs of Nefertari and Amenherkhopshef are of particular interest. Some of the tombs are highly decorated with pictures and hieroglyphs, their colours still surprisingly bright today. At nearby Qurna lies the Valley of the Nobles, with over four hundred tombs in all. At strategic points above them are built the homes of the grave robbers, the villagers who, it may be remembered from the previous chapter, were strangely reluctant to be rehoused!

Aswan is often the most southerly point of the visitor's journey in Egypt, although sometimes excursions are taken to visit the great statues and temples of Abu Simbel further up the Nile. Aswan is a delightful town, a relatively peaceful winter resort full of flowers and blossoming shrubs in season, with a number of river excursions available, including trips to the various islands which lie just across from the main bank of the city. There are botanical gardens on Kitchener's Island; Elephantine Island too has splendid gardens, as well as the ruins of an ancient city built in about 2800

B.C. in honour of the god Khnum. A further island, New Philae, is host to the monuments which were built on the original Philae, an island which was covered by waters from the Aswan Dam. Archaeologists have re-erected here the Temple of Isis, the Temple of Hathor, and various other ancient monuments to preserve them from inundation. Other trips from Aswan include a visit to the ancient granite quarries nearby, and to the desert to savour the tranquillity of the ruined monastery of St Simeon. By contrast, the High Dam is a bleak monument to progress, a controversial masterpiece of modern engineering that has reshaped the Egyptian way of life.

Between Aswan and Luxor lie the towns of Kom Ombo and Edfu, both with important temples. The magnificent shrine at Edfu, dedicated to Horus, is a fine example of late temple building from the Graeco-Roman era. That at Kom Ombo has a fascination for today's visitor, for it was built in honour of the crocodile-headed god Sobek, and crocodile mummies were carefully interred in special tombs there. Some blackened specimens still remain on view for the curious to inspect.

Most trips to Egypt follow the Nile route, but for those who have the time and the opportunity there are other corners of the country to explore. In the Eastern Desert, a barren mountainous region, lie the ancient monasteries of St Anthony and St Paul which still house small communities of monks, and in the Sinai Peninsula there is St Katherine's Monastery, founded in the sixth century on the site where Moses is believed to have received the Ten Commandments from God. From the mountaintop here there is a stunning view across one of the driest and most rugged landscapes on earth.

The Red Sea, it may be surprising to realize, is fast growing in popularity as a holiday area. Some of the best scuba diving in the world is to be found here among the coral reefs, and fishing, boating and camping are also enjoyed by visitors. Hurghada, till recently a modest village, is now the chief tourist resort for the region. At neighbouring el-Ghadarsqa there is an aquarium and museum where the extraordinarily rich marine life of the Red Sea can be studied.

Other noteworthy sites in Egypt abound, and it would take a complete volume to describe them all. Perhaps we should end with Hermopolis Magna, an example of a Graeco-Roman town, now lying in ruins, but, more importantly, the place where the world itself began, according to ancient Egyptian mythology. Here, the primal mound arose from the waters of chaos and the first god, Thoth, the spirit of wisdom, appeared. Then Thoth made the four elements, four divine pairs who were also known as Eternity, Mystery, Night and Darkness. They in turn created an egg, and from this egg was hatched the sun. As the sun was born, a goose flew out of the egg too, and its honking was the first sound heard in the world. Thus Egypt, according to legend, came alive through water, sun, and sound.

Egypt is very much a created country, shaped over the centuries by its inhabitants with extraordinary resourcefulness. Even desert rock and sand have been transformed by their toil into stupendous carvings and fertile soil. In the myth, the land was born from the water, and in one sense this is true, for it is the Nile that has given life to Egypt as we know it. Water comes first in the story, then the sun, whose heat can both parch and fructify, and finally sound — the noise of human life, the interaction of fellow beings who themselves have carried on the work of shaping the land of Egypt over the centuries.

CHRONOLOGY

EARLY DYNASTIC PERIOD
(c.3200-2680 B.C.)

Dynasty I: 3200-2980 B.C.
> Unification of Upper and Lower Egypt under Menes/Narmer
> Menes founds Memphis as the capital
> First Nile dams and canals built

Dynasty II: 2980-2780 B.C.

Dynasty III: 2780-2680 B.C.
> Zoser builds stepped pyramid at Saqqara

OLD KINGDOM
(2680-2258 B.C.)

Dynasty IV: 2680-2565 B.C.
> Pyramids built at Giza by Cheops, Cephren and Mycerinus

Dynasty V: 2565-2420 B.C.

Dynasty VI: 2420-2258 B.C.
> Pepy I wages successful wars against neighbouring lands
> Pepy II reigns for 94 years; central control weakens

FIRST INTERMEDIATE PERIOD
(2258-2052 B.C.)

Dynasty VII: Interregnum (70 kings in 70 days)

Dynasty VIII (Memphite): 2258-2232 B.C.

Dynasty IX (Heracleopolitan): 2232-2140 B.C.

Dynasty X (Heracleopolitan): 2140-2052 B.C.

MIDDLE KINGDOM
(2134-1786 B.C.)

Dynasty XI: 2134-1991 B.C.
> Mentuhotep I and II reunite the country, with Thebes as its capital

Dynasty XII: 1991-1786 B.C.
> Amenemhat I moves the capital to Memphis, extends Egyptian control over Nubia
> Amenemhat III reclaims the Fayyum and builds Bahr el-Yussuf Canal.

SECOND INTERMEDIATE PERIOD
(1786-1570 B.C.)

Dynasties XIII and XIV: 1780-1680 B.C.

Dynasties XV and XVI: 1720-1570 B.C.

Dynasty XVII: 1600-1570 B.C.
> Hyksos invasion

NEW KINGDOM
(1570-1085 B.C.)

Dynasty XVIII: 1570-1314 B.C.
> Ahmose I drives out the Hyksos, makes Thebes his capital
> Tombs built in the Valley of the Kings
> Amenophis (Amenhotep) I reconquers Nubia to the Third Cataract
> Queen Hatshepsut builds her temple at Deir el-Bahari
> Tuthmosis III extends Egypt's empire in Middle East
> Amenophis IV changes his name to Akhenaten, establishes monotheism (worship of Aten, the sun disk) and moves the capital from Thebes to Tell el-Amarna
> General Horemheb assumes power and suppresses the new religion

Dynasty XIX (Ramessidic): 1314-1197 B.C.
> Ramesses II defeats the Hittites, builds colossal monuments throughout the country
> Merenptah defeats the Sea Peoples

Dynasty XX (Ramessidic): 1197-1085 B.C.
> Ramesses III reorganizes the administration, repels the Sea Peoples, builds his funerary temple at Medinet Habu, Thebes

LATE DYNASTIC PERIOD
(1085-332 B.C.)

Dynasty XXI (Tanis and Thebes): 1085-950
> Herihor, first of the priest-kings of Thebes, who share power with the rulers of Tanis in the Delta

Dynasty XXII (Bubastite): 950-730 B.C.
> Sheshonq I sacks Jerusalem

Dynasty XXIII c.817-0730 B.C.

Dynasty XXIV: 730-725 B.C.
> Tef-nekt, prince of Sais, unites the north in the face of the Assyrian threat; Upper Egypt is lost to the Kushite rulers of Nubia (Sudan)

Dynasty XXV (Kushite): 730-656 B.C.
> King Pianky (Piye) of Kush conquers Upper Egypt
> Shabako conquers Lower Egypt
> Esarhaddon, Assyrian emperor, captures Memphis (671 B.C.)
> Ashurbanipal sacks Thebes (663 B.C.)

Dynasty XXVI (Saite): 664-525 B.C.
> Psamtik I drives out the Assyrians (658 B.C.)
> Greek free port of Naukratis founded in the Delta (656 B.C)
> Persian invasion under Cambyses (525 B.C.)

Dynasty XXVII (Persian): 525-404 B.C.
> Cambyses proclaims himself pharaoh; henceforth Persian emperors are sovereigns of Egypt

Dynasties XXVIII, XIX and XXX: 404-341
> Successful revolt against Darius II; Egypt again independent

Dynasty XXI (Persian): 341-332 B.C.
> Fresh Persian invasion drives out Nectanebo II, the last Egyptian pharaoh

MACEDONIAN RULE
(332-304 B.C.)

Alexander the Great of Macedon defeats the Persians and is welcomed by the Egyptians as a liberator
Alexandria founded

THE PTOLEMIES
(305-30 B.C.)

Ptolemy I, one of Alexander's generals, proclaims himself king of Egypt
Temples built at Edfu and Dendera
Cleopatra VII allies herself with Mark Anthony, is defeated at Actium by Octavian (Augustus), and kills herself

ROMAN and BYZANTINE RULE
(30 B.C. - A.D. 640)

Egypt governed by imperial prefects
Emperor Caracalla orders massacre of all adult males of Alexandria (215)
Probus (276-282), first governor of Egypt to become emperor, drives out invading army of Queen Zenobia of Palmyra
St Pachomius founds first Christian monastery near Dendera (c.320)
Edict of Theodosius (392) bans worship of pagan gods
Persian army under Chosroes invades Egypt (616)
Emperor Heraclitus re-establishes Byzantine rule (632)

ISLAMIC ERA

ORTHODOX CALIPHS
(640-661)

Arab conquest of Egypt (639-642) under Amr Ibn el-As, general of Caliph Omar

UMAYYAD CALIPHS (in Damascus)
(661-750)

Arabic made the offical language

ABBASIDS (in Baghdad)
(750-868)

TULUNIDS
(868-905)

Sultan Tulun founds a new Turkish dynasty in Cairo, builds mosque of Ibn Tulun

IKHSHIDS
(935-969)

Sultan Mohammed Tughi (Ikhshid) carries out agricultural reforms; the arts flourish in his reign

FATIMIDS
(969-1171)

General Gohar founds the city of el-Qahira (Cairo), and in 972 completes el-Azhar mosque, where an Islamic university is founded (988)

AYYUBIDS
(1171-1250)

Saladin (Salah el-Din) founds a Kurdish dynasty, wins glory in the wars against the Crusaders, builds the Cairo Citadel

MAMLUK RULE
(1250-1517)

Bahri (Turkish) Mamluks: 1250-1382
Buryi (Circassian) Mamluks: 1328-1517
Ottoman Sultan Selim I defeats Mamluks near Aleppo (1516)

OTTOMAN RULE
(1517-1768)

Istanbul replaces Cairo as the leading city of Islam, Egypt governed by pashas

1768	Ali Bey refuses to pay tribute to the Sultan, Mamluk rule re-established
1798	Napoleon lands in Egypt; his army wins the Battle of the Pyramids, and he establishes control over the country
1801	The French, defeated by the British, withdraw
1805-1847	Mehmet (Mohammed) Ali, nominated pasha by the Sultan, unites the country, breaks the power of the Mamluks, and carries out wide reforms; his line rules Egypt until 1952
1859	Construction of Suez Canal begun with French financing
1863-1879	Rule of Ismail Pasha, granted the title of khedive in 1867
1869	Opening of Suez Canal
1882	Britain establishes its rule by military intervention
1922	Egypt declared an independent country, but Britain retains a military presence
1923	Constitution makes Egypt a parliamentary democracy with a monarch, King Fuad I, son of Khedive Ismail
1952	Revolution led by Free Officers dethrones King Farouk
1953	Egypt proclaimed a republic
1953-1954	Presidency of General Mohammed Naguib
1954-1970	Presidency of Gamal Abdel Nasser
1956	Suez Canal nationalized; Franco-British military intervention checked by United Nations action; British troops finally leave Egypt
1967	Egypt, Syria and Jordan attack Israel and are defeated in the Six-Day War
1970-1981	Presidency of Anwar el-Sadat
1973	Yom Kippur War with Israel restores Egyptian pride
1979	Camp David accord signed with Israel
1981	President Sadat assassinated by Islamic extremists; Hosni Mubarak elected president
1987	President Mubarak re-elected for six-year term

Note: Ancient Egyptian dating is still subject to scholarly debate. Not all authorities will agree with the dating adopted here.

Index